The Zen
of Weight Loss

Karen Fili Sullivan
Jeri Levesque, Ed.D.

The Zen
of Weight Loss

A Mindful, Livable Approach to Fitness

Karen Fili Sullivan
Jeri Levesque, Ed.D.

ISBN-13: 978-1978215023
ISBN-10: 1978215029

ZWL

For the men in my life, David, Brenden, and Jared.
Also my parents, Walt and Gloria Fili.
Then a cast of thousands who've worked
with me toward fitness and enlightenment–
Not necessarily in that order. A dedication
seems trite after all you have given me,
But here it is–with love.

~ Karen

To my grandkids, present and coming–
that you will know health and fitness as treasures
worth far more than wealth because they come
with the power to shape your life and the children
of your futures.

~ Jeri

Acknowledgements

We would like to thank the people who helped us get this work to the public. To our editor, Amberley Doskey, thanks for all your time editing and removing the 100 references to "folks." For our designer/proof reader Susan Ormston. Your development of the look for *ZWL* was more perfect than we could have imagined. The work you both did kept us from rewriting until 2025. Thank you very much.

We were fortunate enough to find several photos which carried the *ZWL* theme. They grace the pages at the beginning of each section, and are the work of photographer Vona G. Broughton, MHS, CHES, RYT. (www.facebook.com/vonabphotography). Her models are listed alphabetically:

- Colleen Kirkpatrick. Runner and Yogi, Co-Founder of *The Soul Shine Project* (www.facebook.com/thesoulshineproject)

- Whitney Messervy, yogini

- Susan Ward, Broker in Charge, RYT. Sue Ward Homes. Iyengar Yoga Student (www.suewardhomes.com)

- Rindi Wood, yogini

We appreciate their willingness to be part of this publication. They're a perfect fit for *ZWL*, and their energy has added a special dimension to this work.

> *"When you realize how perfect everything is you will tilt your head back and laugh at the sky."*
>
> ~ *Buddha*

Contents

Zen

Weight

Loss

ZWL Plan

Appendix

Zen

"The most important point is to accept yourself and stand on your two feet."

~ Shunryu Suzuki

Now and Zen

There is nothing better than a fit body. Are you on a quest for a healthier, thinner body? No matter where you look headlines promise the solution you've been seeking. Your disappointment grows as you realize they're all reading from the same script. No matter how you spin it, weight loss books are the same. They tell you to eat less and exercise more.

The fact is—they're right. Why then, is it that a huge percentage of the population still struggles with obesity after multiple attempts at dieting and exercising? Why can't this scientific fact work for you?

We believe that most diet plans don't take into consideration your history with dieting, or your emotional attachment to food. Not to mention how little time or money you have to get proper exercise and healthy food. The fundamental issue with diets and weight loss programs is that they belong to someone else. The missing piece to the puzzle is how to convert the science of "eat less, exercise more" to fit your life. This is what we teach our readers; how to take ownership of your health and fitness.

Follow the outline and build a program that will be a good fit for you.

We call our method the *Zen of Weight Loss* or ZWL. It's not religion. We aren't theologians nor are we here to convert you to Eastern beliefs or philosophies. We find value in the practice of Zen because it's about focus, calmness and enlightenment. We do this without ignoring the science of mind, brain, and body. Next, we connect the Zen method of mindfulness to weight loss to bring you closer to your fitness goal. From a passage in an unpretentious little book by Chris Prentiss we found a simple explanation of Zen;

> "The Zen of doing anything is doing it with a particular concentration of mindfulness, a calmness and simplicity of mind that brings the experience of enlightenment and, through that experience, happiness." (from Zen and the Art of Happiness)

The Zen of Weight Loss is exercising and eating with a calmness and simplicity of mind that brings forth fitness, a lean healthy body, and ultimately, achieving your goal in ways that foster happiness. We are not suggesting that an ideal weight alone is responsible for happiness. When your body reflects a healthy lifestyle you will feel better! Our program is a way to tame unhealthy desires that are closely associated with being out of shape, overweight, and obese. We advocate for fitness and wellness—two attachments linked with healthy lifestyles. The Zen approach accentuates the primary connections between our brains and minds, emotions and behavior, body and health. The term *fitness* reflects the goal of this program that you enjoy a robust lifestyle for many years to come. The Zen experience is the joyful awareness of being full-bodied, strong, and well.

Zen as a Way

Buddhism has its roots within the Hindu culture in India. Prince Siddhartha Gautama was born in at Lumbini near Nepal in 563 BC. Though much loved as a child, Siddhartha grew up to be restless and troubled with self-doubt. As a young man he left the royal trappings of his family in search of spiritual truth and the cause of human suffering. After much meditation he became known as the Buddha, a name that means "the enlightened one" or "awakened". Buddha's teachings traveled to China, Vietnam, Korea and Japan, and more schools of thought were developed. After the year 845 two main Zen schools emerged—Lin-chi and Ts'ao-tung. The Lin-chi places greater emphasis on *koans*, paradoxical or nonsensical questions designed to suddenly bring enlightenment, and effort to attain enlightenment. *Koans* trigger rapid enlightenment in students by shocking them out of their conventional ways of logical thinking. That's part of the ZWL workout program—to zap your neural pathways with new connections that make it easier to think your way to actions that reconstruct a sleek and fit body.

ZWL deals with developing a better understanding of yourself and the world relative to fitness. Rather than a simple workout protocol, we discuss how thoughts and emotions control people's actions and either support or sabotage everyone's relationships with food and exercise.

Zen is a discipline. It is a philosophical approach to living and finding understanding. Zen can be practiced during quiet moments when you close your eyes and reflect. It is a way to sing with the universe in silence. Within the silent spaces we become mindful of our motivations and actions. The ZWL is an orientation to changes within your brain and body that will become the "one-point" of your healthy identity.

Listening To Self

Every choice you make has a consequence. Speeding can get you a traffic citation, but when you're late for an appointment you may choose to gamble and floor the accelerator. When you choose to eat chocolate cake instead of fruit for dessert, the resulting weight gain is a natural consequence of that decision. Bad food choices are exacerbated by our fast paced lifestyles. We don't have time to eat a meal, taste food, and talk with our loved ones. The screaming din of life in the fast lane won't allow you to hear yourself think, let alone hear about your spouse's day.

The baby boomers have experienced great changes during their lifetimes. Baby Boomers Jeri and Karen are both proud members! Our summers included walks on the beach, trips to the State Fair, and running from yard to yard playing games with silly names. Our children attended camps, swim team and baseball practices, and the library reading challenge. All good for growing well balanced children—but very busy and often orchestrated by parents. Today's generation is inundated with technology that has them spending far too much time warming the seat of their pants. But, how does this translate to weight issues?

Our life schedules take priority over healthy choices. Work, school and activities leave no time for food preparation. The drive-through is convenient choice because the alternative takes too much time. Food preparation and cooking are becoming lost arts. It takes a strong person to plant your feet and say, *enough!* Weight loss starts with changing the pace of your life.

Change isn't going to happen overnight. It's imperative to modify your lifestyle through a centered mindset to achieve your desires for fitness and appearance. Start with listening to the best coach in the room—the one holding this book. Your weight loss journey starts with being aware of your surroundings.

Awareness

This exercise in awareness is easy. Human beings can't turn their brains off, and for this exercise you'll need a mind that's ready to work. You'll also need a notebook or piece of paper to make notes. Find a quiet place where you won't be disturbed. Turn off the phone. Start a timer for one minute. Become aware of your surroundings. Do you feel a breeze? Hear a dog barking or the buzz of a fly? Make notes regarding this experience.

Listen:

"Did I just hear a dog bark?...I can't believe they left Fido out in all this heat!...Hot, it's so hot today. It's Tuesday, I have a haircut next Tuesday.... Hair, wonder if I should go lighter... I feel light.... I want to lose weight.... That dog barking again?"

This is a perfect example of what the Buddha called the Monkey Mind. We call it hop-scotching with your thoughts. The game goes on until you stop to pick up your stone and then you take off again. The pause you take in your mind is probably as short a time as it would take you to pick up a stone in a real game of hop scotch, but with practice that time gets longer and longer. The mind wanders less.

The Buddha observed people and understood how the mind works. Sociologist, B.J. Gallagher calls the Buddha, "the smartest psychologist she's ever read." She explains, "...(He) wasn't a god or a messiah—he was simply a very wise teacher with keen insights into human nature..."[1] The mind will jump around, but it can be controlled through focusing your attention on one thing. Breathe! It's a simple, not fancy, mechanism for focusing. In daily life you can practice by being mindful.

---

1 See www.huffingtonpost.com/bj-gallagher/buddha-how-to-tame-your-m_b_945793.html

Mindfulness is the practice of awareness of your environment, body and mind. The unspoken benefit of paying attention to things is learning by experience. This isn't a foreign concept, although you may not have called it mindfulness. Your mother told you to pay attention all your life, "Watch when you cross the street, look both ways, pay attention to the teacher, and watch the other players on the basketball court so you know where you can throw the ball." It's all mindfulness.

We will take mindfullness a step further and ask you to take short breaks throughout the day and be attentive to your every response to the world. As with the experiment we did earlier, having a calm mind is important for everyday living and your success of the ZWL program.

Where to Start

Begin with making no assumptions, theories or predictions about how ZWL going to come out. The results will be directly proportional to the amount of work you devote. Every action has a consequence. So, blame no one—not even yourself. Own up to the fact that you are at the helm of this vessel and are the one in control. Drive right into a routine of introspection. Spend time with yourself every day. In a perfect world you can sit right down for 30-minutes perhaps twice a day. In reality, you will be fortunate to be comfortable with 2 to 10 minutes each day. Begin, proceed, observe the journey rather than be distracted by imagining the destination.

Find a more comfortable place to sit than where you were in the first experiment. We will be working for 10 minutes this time. We recommend you sit rather than lie down so you won't fall asleep, but don't worry if you do fall asleep. Nothing here is forced. Begin by being kind and respecting your body and mind. Remember, this is a practice session, an experiment in discovering how to calm the mind. There is no good or bad to becoming mindful; it just is.

Calming the mind starts with watching your breath. Breath—the essence of life is central to finding a calm place for your mind. Start with a dry run. As you read this text allow yourself to do what the text suggests. Once we are done, put the book down, and begin to breathe.

- Notice how the air is cool as it goes in…warmed by your lungs as it comes out.

- Feel your chest expand on the inhale, collapse on the exhale.

- Make your belly fill with air, contract to push the air out.

- Do your shoulders rise as you inhale? Do they stay up on the exhale or relax?

For the 10 minutes you may have discovered you were only able to think about your breath for 3 seconds at a time. You'll have found your mind was elsewhere with no idea how it came to be so far from your breath. This is normal and expected. You may have several thoughts before you stop them from running amuck. Once you see thoughts marching through your mind, acknowledge them, and then gently lead your mind back to your breathing. The mind will keep working and drift away from the breath, but you can always lead it back to where you started. Keep doing it until the timer sounds. Set time aside to meditate daily. Meditation is a practice which improves when repeated regularly.

You may wonder how this can ever do anything for your weight loss! Mindful breathing alone won't make you lose weight, but it should lead to an awareness of your body. Eventually, you will associate the awareness with the food consumed during any given day. Compulsion and immediate gratification are thoughtless acts of unkindness. Persuasions are responsible for decisions to snag dinner through the fast food lane or eat your children's leftovers after eating a full meal. That cycle of "snatch and gobble" will fade with a mindful approach toward preparing and eating food.

Zen Practiced Here

While the practice of mindfulness is perfected through meditation, ZWL doesn't require meditation to succeed. It's good sense to become attentive, aware, and careful about what you do today. This is more than making decisions about what you will eat. Start by being aware of everything around you. Have you ever left the grocery store to realize you never made eye contact with the cashier? How you relate to people around you will change. After practicing breathing for a couple of weeks, how you feel about yourself will be different. Through this introspection you'll discover a whole new YOU!

Blaze a Path

You're not going to have to wade through dense, technical diagrams showing how muscle fiber reacts to specific resistance programs in this book. *The Zen of Weight Loss* is a path to travel toward health and fitness. Karen has successfully guided scores of clients along this path every day for the last 20 years.

We all recognize vicious patterns that take us away from the path and lose us to unhealthy wanderings. One key to breaking a destructive pattern of body neglect is to evaluate weight loss advertisements and prescriptions that clog the mass media. Reject weight loss messages that state how easy it is to lose weight and gain a perfect figure—FAST. A thin body isn't necessarily healthy. If people have to break basic "rules" of physiology to get thin they aren't doing themselves any favors.

Fitness is a goal that will last for the rest of your life with a minimal financial investment. *The Zen of Weight Loss* plan can help you master your fitness goals. You are probably spending more than the cost of a book already on special food, exercise equipment, supplements, or gym memberships—without reaching your goals. Give this approach to mindfulness, fitness, wellbeing and health a chance.

Illuminate

Let's not limit our journey to words of advice. Listen to your own inner voice. Start keeping a daily journal. Include notes on how much and what you eat. Journals are where we are free to express our feelings and fears as well as triumphs and pleasures.

The way you write about your journey is personal. Jeri's husband, George has kept running logs for 40 years. Sometimes he'll sit up in bed reading entries. He is saving them as memoirs to his pursuit of weight control and fitness. His May 1993 his entry reads,

"St. Chas. w/RP 2 loops w/o river walk. OK. 3.75 40.24".

Translation: he's home, went running with his best friend Ralph P., jogged 2 loops at the park, didn't go to the river, ran 3.75 miles in 40 minutes, 24 seconds.

Ten years later he is no more poetic,

"St Chas, KD wdn bdg OK stiff 3.3, 41.50."

He's back home, on the Katy Trail by the river, he went over the bridge. He feels okay but stiff during his 3.3 mile run/jog that he did a bit faster a decade ago.

Get the drift? What matters about a journal is what it means to you. George's log entries consistently report location, date, distance, physical condition, and total lapsed time of his exercise routine. His log style hardly varies over 40 years because it's his ticket to anywhere he wants to go.

You can learn to understand your body by what you have written. We process much of what we know through emotions. It's how our brains are wired so that we hold new learning in memory for a long time. Put your index finger across your eye and stretch your thumb to the side of your head. That's where deep in your brain sits a grape-size structure, the amygdala, which filters most of what we perceive through an emotional network that's wired across all of the nervous system. Humans learn by processing information through this neural center with a simple sorting system: "good—like it—do it often" or "bad—hate it—avoid."

We have special place in memory for much of what we process as "very good, wonderful" and "downright awful and scary." You'll want to keep track of how you emotionally filter food even when you *know* it's not good in your journal. Be honest. You're not writing a blog or Facebook entry, this is personal. What word or phrase comes to mind as you're eating? What word describes your feelings after eating? Later we'll talk about the conflict of feelings that arise when the entry before eating says, "deliriously delicious" and after the meal entry reads, "depressed and bloated."

Let's update the path metaphor and get on some asphalt for a bit. Drivers learn quickly that failure to pay attention to road signs and traffic lights can be fatal. You might get away with running a red light one day only to be broadsided by a semi-trailer the next. Keeping a journal is one of the key secrets of the elite group of folks who set weight-loss goals, meet and maintain them. Think of it as a traffic-control. Your journal will be a smart GPS that lets you know the current condition of your body and where the road hazards lie.

Most people who set goals that involve physical and emotional change yet avoid recording their thoughts and feelings eventually revert back to the way they were before the changes occurred! Being part of the "Elite 15%" of the "lean and be seen" means paying attention to the road.

You'll find several charts at the end of this book designed to help outline key questions that only you can answer in your personal quest for fitness. Get a 5"×7" spiral bound notebook for recording your changing thoughts about your changing body. You can title your notebook as "Dear Diary" if it conjures up good feelings about keeping your best secrets locked in a vinyl binding protected a tiny shiny key.

Keeping records is important. Think about that grape-sized emotional sentinel in your brain. We tend to remember things that trigger high emotional responses—good or bad—and not bother to clutter our memory banks with things that have less impact. Most folks eat at least three times a day, throw in a snack and they are challenged to remember 1,460 meals a year! This is a heavy memory load.

The U.S. Department of Agriculture estimates that the average person in the United States eats .5 lbs of meat, 1.6 lbs of dairy products, .2 lbs of fats and oils, 1.9 lbs of fruits and vegetables, .5 lbs of grains, and .4 lbs of sugars per day for a total of *4.7 lbs of food per day*.[2] Nobody should be expected to remember how much food or how many different thoughts and feelings affected you a week ago.

Use the *Zen* worksheets as a template or design your own way of keeping records. The point is—write it out.

One approach to losing weight or getting in shape is to go to a gym and find a trainer. There is a plethora of coaches and personal trainers. From the guy or gal in your local gym to television trainers, anyone can find the right trainers to help them develop and stick with fitness regimens.

Step Forward

For the most part, trainers know and understand the basics of exercise and nutrition. Some have bachelor or master degrees behind their certifications, but the other end of the spectrum includes people who claim to be trainers and have no formal training.

2 To see the USDA report, visit www.usda.gov/factbook/chapter2.htm

So whom do you trust? Simple answer, the best person you can trust is you. This book is a way of teaching you to be your own go-to person. Learn how to sort through the nonsense you're fed regarding health, fitness and weight loss. Find success with the program *you* are going to design as a Zen-Now way of staying fit.

Seems like a tall order. Have faith in yourself and your ability to learn how to be the designer of your own changes. You will find the deepest most private reason why you want to get fit and thin. Then you will set your goals small and large but always reasonable.

We're going to discuss the ways your *mind-body* works. We'll dispute fabrications about food and dieting. You'll overcome excuses. You will find support to make life changes that will change you for better *and* for good. These changes will happen as you adopt three levels of workouts designed to frame your personal exercise routine.

We share similar stories. At one time or another many of us tried over and over to get "this weight off" only to fail. It's hard to feel the glow of positive self-esteem when looking at a track record like that. Start fresh! Think Success! Exceed and survive! Join us for the long haul. We are going to show you *how* to change for better and good by designing a program you can live with and thrive. Don't be like Scarlet O'Hara by saying, "Fiddle de dee!" and try to put it off until tomorrow. Take charge today and call your own shots for a truly successful fitness experience.

Let's get started on that body you never thought you would have but will find just a ways down the path. Think bright. This is your enlightenment.

"To a mind that is still,
the whole universe surrenders."

~ Chuang-tzu

2

Brains Matter in Fitness

"If you cannot find the truth right where you are, where else do you expect to find it?"

~ Chuang-tzu

It's a natural part of being human to hang onto and protect the things that we claim to own. In order to lose weight, you're going to let go of some extra pounds. Zen of Weight Loss (ZWL) is a way to focus on messages received daily about weight loss and fitness so that you don't get attached to quick fix gimmicks. Instead, you're going to focus and make reasonable decisions about what you eat, how much you exercise, and how you mindfully live moment-to-moment, day-by-day.

Defeat Criticism

Let us agree that there is never an excuse for hurting another human being. Unfortunately, somewhere along the way, it seems that obese people got left out of the Golden Rule. We may have observed two different reactions of others to an obese person at a shopping mall, disgust or pity. Living with this kind of social pressure from society drives one to believe what others think, no matter how heartless and judgmental.

Defeating one's self-esteem surrenders personal will to the self-fulfilling prophecy. Why wallow in puddles of self-loathing instead of focusing on the esteem of your goodness? Choose not to give control to care-less people who could better spend their energy looking in their own mirrors.

Your body is not about "being fat." Your weight *problem* isn't because you are fat. Thin people might think it's because you have no willpower, or you like wearing extra large clothes. They'll never be able to know your struggle. But why give them your struggle? It's *yours* to conquer. Your path, your story—it doesn't belong to anyone else.

Imagine what happens if you say to yourself, "It's too hard to lose weight! I haven't got the discipline. I don't have time to work out. I'll just have to live with a fat body." You will make conscious decisions to protect this identity you've created. You're trapped in your own imagination. These statements reflect deeply personal feelings that Buddha called, "attachments." You need to learn to better deal with your feelings rather than push them to the back of your mind. Suppressed feelings are like Styrofoam in a landfill—they never go away and cannot be recycled into something good.

What we often feel is frustration that the task of losing weight is difficult and not easy. We feel threatened by the potential for failing with yet another program or pouch of pills. We become angry when our appetite reels out of control. At this point you feel a great longing to be slimmer, fitter and happier. But how can we make our wishes come true?

Not all, but many thin people conclude that willpower alone is the missing factor in weight loss. That leads to a chain of thoughts based on lazy logic, "if you are fat it's because you just don't want to use your willpower—because you're lazy." Fat and lazy are pejorative terms meant to hurt. We'll talk more about the power emotions have on learning about anything in the world. Later you'll learn to tap your emotions rather than tamper with them.

As for willpower—it is like a muscle. You develop willpower by exercising willpower. You have to engage in disciplined training and rigorous practice with positive mindfulness to be better able to resist your own natural impulses. This is a core tenet of ZWL.

Rev up that little grape-sized bundle of neurons in your brain (call it by name, it's your amygdala) and that deep seeded soul of emotions known as the limbic system. Render negative input as "not worth thinking about, feel nothing, remember nothing. No room in the memory bin!" If you start building on negative beliefs you will take flight from the problem rather than restrict or augment your diet. You'll become your worst fears; too lazy to exercise and too lazy to care.

The saying "the buck stops here" doesn't mean grab a dollar and buy a donut. From a ZWL perspective, your worst enemy cannot harm you worse than your own unguarded thoughts. Think good thoughts and be at peace.

Overcoming

Karen struggles with an eating disorder. She is what she eats. No excuses for her, but after having weighed 290 for a long time her weight is down about a hundred pounds. She struggles with the additional weight while working with clients who get thin and sleek. They are wonderful to work with as she works to practice what she preaches.

At one dark time of her life, Karen sought out health care professionals who did tests like hair analysis to identify issues she hoped to control and then lead to a dramatic weight loss. She analyzed and poked holes in numerous weight loss programs and deemed them "un-liveable." These frustrations led to the development of the ZWL program.

An "un-liveable" diet or fitness routine is something you cannot do for longer than it takes you to drop excess weight. A quick fix is a guarantee to recycle fat. Throw it away and it boomerangs right back. ZWL advocates for healthy approaches that compel focus and attention to what you are doing at this very moment to be slim and fit.

Be realistic and balance your commitment to fitness. Sign up for six days a week regimen of cardio and a diet of rice crackers and celery and you can skip the palm reader. The future will find your body right back where you started. Start small and make changes because you KNOW how much better it will be for you.

Fit Brains

Brains also work toward their own goals. Whatever ZWL changes you make to your exercise and diet, be sure they are changes you can live with over time. Otherwise, the brain will slip back into its own favorite and comfortable patterns. Brains are pattern makers that take pleasure in ordering chaotic information. One of the primary goals of ZWL is to find a sustainable weight loss and fitness strategy.

Pattern making creates meaning. We must teach our brains to demand regular, rigorous exercise and good nutrition. Brains love meaningful stuff. That's what the ZWL provides thorough explanations of how the brain and body are primed or harmed by movement, diet, and the environment.

It's essential to teach our brains to make healthy food choices. We have to snag the brain's attention. We have about 18 seconds of focus before drifting if something is just not that interesting. Grocery shopping and meal preparation are ways to trigger multiple brain centers to process information. Fresh ripe tomatoes with a pungent scent, vivid color, and heft trigger our appetite. The sizzle of fajitas on a cast iron skillet and the aroma of garlic sautéing in extra virgin olive oil prepare our brain for pleasurable dining.

Metabolic Changes

The brain controls a number of overlapping systems that it can command to help you keep your weight off. It has about a dozen neurotransmitters that can signal the body to pack on some pounds and just as many to tell it to trim down. Notice here the brain has a built in sense of "appropriate" that your mind is going to have to rewire.

You can change your brain's sense of what's appropriate by resetting your metabolic rate to "high." A half an hour of vigorous exercise can boost your metabolism by 20-30% and keep it grinding off excess calories for up to 15 hours. Eating breakfast everyday also kick starts the daily metabolic rate.

Calculating a body's metabolism is complicated. It requires determining how many calories your body burns at rest. Severely low calorie diets never work in the long run because brains protect their bodies from starvation. A person in the throngs of a severe weight loss diet will have a slower metabolism. The brain tells the body to hold off burning up the few calories that pass through. This is why when someone abandons the sawdust-and-spit diet and resumes regular eating they are shocked at how quickly lost weight finds its way back again. A body that has been in starvation mode will cling to calories as if they were life preservers. It takes awhile for the metabolism to reset to a higher rate after running on low.

The passing of time is no ally of metabolism. As we age, our metabolism tends to slow down. We maintain the mind world connection that the things we loved to eat as teens are burned off just as fast when we show our AARP card to get the "blue hair" dinner special. The "ten for ten" axiom refers to the tendency for middle-aged people to gain a pound a year. This is why few of us can fit into our wedding outfits at our 25th anniversary gala.

Shhhhh…

It's also important to sleep. Yes, when it comes to weight, you *can* sleep it off. Sleep deprivation slams the breaks on the metabolism. We are a sleep-deprived society where nearly a third of adults report sleeping less than seven hours a night compared to the nine hours that their great grandparents snoozed. We are pushing our waking selves to the limits by severely disrupting the equilibrium of our hormones and metabolism.[3] The impact of sleep disorders is recognized as a contributing factor to obesity and diabetes. Since most of us struggle to maintain an ideal weight over time, even when we adhere to healthy eating and regular exercise, the importance of sleep cannot be ignored.

Burning the candle at both ends leaves us exhausted and cranky. We become stressed out—and sometimes food seems to be the only source of comfort. That's because the lack of sleep increased our brain's level of cortisol. That's the substance the fuels the quick response to take flight or stand and fight—which makes us feel hungry. Extra food spikes our sugar levels and stymies our bodies' ability to metabolize carbohydrates. Darn the 24/7 demands of the 21st century—we're left with higher insulin levels and more fat storage. And even worse, groggy and addled we crave more carbs and a nap we don't have time to take. Sleep is clearly a critical component of the ZWL approach to fitness.

---

3 Sunil Sharma and Mani Kavuru, *Sleep and Metabolism: An Overview.* Available online at http://www.hindawi.com/journals/ije/2010/270832/

Move to Lose

Brains learn best when they are connected directly to physical experience. They have a deep and profound love of music. This explains why exercise is enhanced with heart pumping music in the room or plugged into your ears during a long run down the trail.

There are many ways the brain rewards exercise. If you are physically active, it's more likely you'll eat reasonable portions of healthy foods. We teach our brains meaningful fitness patterns by keeping weekly workout cycles and journaling. It's essential to snag the brain's attention so that it can focus on details.

Brains are learning machines. To keep them fit we have to develop new skills through out our lifetime. Brains prefer challenges that command their full attentions. ZWL pampers brains with a progressive program. Exercises proceed from easy to hard and simple to complex by levels of experience.

Comfort Stress

In order to lose weight and become fit you're going to sweat your brains out and adopt a healthy diet. That is a demanding challenge. Brains learn best when faced with a balance of stress and comfort. They like situations that have a high challenge associated with a low threat. You can work for an hour with a physical trainer and be secure knowing you won't be pushed past your endurance level to the point of getting hurt. The combination of stress and comfort activates emotions. It's through emotions that learning and the capacity to remember our lessons become indelible.

Stress stimulates a survival imperative. There are parts of ZWL that are intended to elevate your stress level. There are disturbing facts to consider about the effects of mass marketing and obesity that should make you feel uncomfortable. When the brain senses too little stress it becomes too comfortable and relaxed to be actively engaged in skill building. Our readers would easily ignore our suggestions for regular exercise, mindfulness, and good nutrition.

You need to teach your brains the elements and actions of fitness and weight loss by sparking emotional interest. That's why ZWL endorses dining celebrations and rituals as well as daily exercise and meditation. You'll create safe environments to learn and practice these new skills and orientation to the good life.

Pain for Gain

Adages such as "no pain no gain" reflect certain non-negotiable constructs about weight loss that appeal to our brains. When the brain feels discomfort in the body's joints and muscles after a demanding workout, it interprets these sensations as evidence that a challenge was conquered. The brain floods itself with endorphins, powerful chemicals that reward it with a flush of pleasure. The second wind and runner's high are the brain's way of applauding the body for hard effort and good work.

Learning fitness acts like a vaccine. It will boost your mental powers and protect your body from bad choices. Our weight loss intelligence is flexible and subject to great change.

Flow

Visualize mounting a treadmill and setting the machine at a brisk pace. The earplugs are tucked in and the iPod is tuned to a favorite playlist. You begin walking. You body moves in sync with the rhythm of the song. You feel the pulse of the machine and beat of your heart. Your legs pump energy into the rolling path beneath your flying feet. Your senses are focused on breathing, the way your arms seem to swing in perfect rhythm to the beat of the song and your heart keeps a steady beat as you continue to run.

You become completely immersed in the moment as each step pushes you further. You forget what's playing on the iPod and begin to imagine excess weight melting off your hips. Muscles seem to glisten with new strength. You sense blood flowing throughout your body and energy blazing within your mind. Aches fade as tiny beads of sweat affirm a total immersion with the moment.

This intense focus was termed "flow" by psychologist Mihaly Csiksentimhalyi.[4] He explains flow as the positive psychology of being completely involved in an activity for its own sake. These are optimal experiences when we feel in complete control of our actions. You do simply to do. The sense of time fades as every action sets the stage for the next. Your senses are completely focused on the task at hand. You are in the zone; concentrated, serene, and in control. You tackle difficult challenges with your own effort and resolve. When flow happens we feel complete exhilaration. Memories of experiences will take us to an unconscious state of being. During flow, we do for the sake of doing.

Csiksentimhalyi believes that these prized moments are neither passive nor relaxing. Rather the best moments of flow happen when our minds and bodies are stretched to their limits. ZWL sets high expectations that you can and will make life lasting changes in your body and mind that will bring forth the joy of fitness. We want you to go with the flow from being out of shape to the optimal experience of being a fine tuned mind-body.

The World is Brain Food

Mental stimulation, in the long run, is as essential to the body as food. The brain uses experience to wire itself. It uses the world during optimal growth phases to create certain specialized cells

---

4 Cskisentimhalyi's book *Flow* is available on line at http://www.amazon.com/Flow-Psychology-Experience-Mihaly-Csikszentmihalyi/dp/0061339202. There are also YouTube videos of the author explaining positive psychology and flow.

and connections that generate mass and energy. Thoughout its life span, the brain builds new pathways that enable it to better adapt to change.

Knowledge about the world stored chemically and electronically between our ears is as real to the brain as fresh experiences gathered from the world in a given moment. The brain can't distinguish between the reality of dreams and actual life experience. The brain holds dear knowledge that assures its safety. Brains want the content of its life experience to be positive, meaningful, and emotionally satisfying.

Mendacities

3

"To a mind that is still, the whole universe surrenders."

~ *Chuang-tzu*

The "mad men" of the marketing industry manipulate an essential human weakness that evolved during the media age; people trust information transmitted through television, magazines, and the Internet. Strong people avoid becoming co-dependent partners of advertisers. The American public is maneuvered through a web of opinions and studies regarding health, fitness, and weight loss. We're going to talk about the underside of the fitness and weight loss industries that are branded by deceptions, falsehoods, and inaccuracies. The point is, we need to practice diverting our attention away from weight-loss ploys so that we can make reasonable decisions about fitness.

Commercial producers that make big bucks hawking false pathways to weight loss are aggravating. Just take a quick peek at what's available online about the subject of weight loss. Today's browser search generated 106,000,000 hits for weight loss and 33,600,000 listings for weight loss exercise. We are experiencing what Alvin Toffler back in the 1970s called "Future Shock". We have a lot of information but very little understanding, and even less wisdom. Because there is so much information, many people simply back off and grab the closest or quickest answer to a problem rather than think it through. Think about what we already know relative to our bodies. Next, let's figure out what to change and then realistically lay out a plan.

Distract and Net

Internet web pages are designed to distract. Windows pop up with ads that continuously pop up with a flash and a beep to catch attention. The Internet is an interruption system that creates cognitive surplus—there is too much information to absorb. The portal between the working memory—which is fragile and fleeting—and long term memory is clogged with more information that it can sort for storage. The more a person skims and scans multiple email accounts, social media updates and instant messages the less this information is deemed worth keeping.

We are to a great extent the product of what we read and how we read. Humans are not born readers. They teach their brains to make meaning from printed language. When the bulk of reading experiences are web-based interactions, the mind learns to weave different circuits from what's new on the page with what it already knows. People have the innate ability to literally build new circuits in their brains that are designed for the Internet. These neural pathways are distinct from those woven by reading books.

Distractions and limited demands for extended concentration let the brain get used to attending minimally to information on its scratch pad of working memory. This information is forgotten rather than stored carefully for later use.

Net ads seize our attention and compel us to make decisions based on negligible information. For example an email pops up with a sales notice for a digital book; up flashes an icon of the book cover and a box marked *Buy*. Within moments you've got a new book in your library. Sales exchanges like these rewire the brain to attend to more quick-slick sales gimmicks that we don't have time to think about in a deep or coherent manner.

The intention of this book is to help you discern the mis-information crowding the Internet, stuffing your mailbox, and weighing you down. With the Zen approach you'll become more self-reliant and in control of the changes you make for your mind-body. You are going to take ownership of the body on the path, the path, and the destinations you reach from here forward. You will reach your goal in a manner that is reasonable and healthy.

Misleading

Some information is crafted to look like it's based on scientific studies done by well-respected experts at famous research facilities. The messages implied by this "research" are written to look like medical facts. And, as we know, a fact is more than just information; it is the truth or reality of something. We believe some advertisements really are the real deal and those products the answer to our prayers. Wait! Caveat emptor! Buyers beware! Some of these ads are no more than propaganda, half-truths fashioned to influence and control consumers' thinking. They are created as a marketing tool called positioning. The sole purpose of the "research" is to influence consumers.

The mis-direction doesn't stop here. You've probably seen full-page "true life stories" on the Internet or in magazines. They're also advertisements disguised to look like applied research in the form of new, much needed products. You've probably considered ordering whatever they're pushing. It's hard to believe that the person in the article's photo is a professional model. Better yet, the story was written to target people who, based on prior life experiences (such as being overweight and under-fit), can be convinced that they need to buy that product right now!

This is Not Wonderland

The movies are the only place where you can take a little pill and your world changes—completely. You can't gorge yourself on cheeseburgers and morph into a thin body. You can't expect to exercise less, eat more, and live long.

Look at the media flood of messages that scream at us about weight loss:

no fat

no carbs

lower protein

this diet, that diet

take a pill

drink vinegar

don't drink vinegar

eat lots, eat less

see a shrink

blame your mother

good fats, bad fats

it's a hormone problem!

it's genetic; all your family is fat.

Despite the hype, America is glutted with pudgy people. Fat not fit is the norm. A recent Gallup-Healthways Well-Being Index found that over 55.1%% of Americans describe themselves as overweight or obese![5] We are becoming corpulent people in a diverse nation of plus sizes. At the same time, about half of the country's children

---

5 In the U.S., Majority Overweight or Obese in All 50 States, Retrieved on line at http://www.gallup.com/poll/156707/majority-overweight-obese-states.aspx

are on free and reduced school lunch. Many of these children who live in poverty are already obese and suffer from diabetes.

Some of the recommended "treatments" for obesity just compound the problem. As we said earlier, radical diets with severely limited caloric intake reset the metabolism at a lower level and cause the body to conserve the few calories it takes in and crave larger portions when the diet is abandoned. Diets calling for an imbalance of food groups disrupt the symbiotic relationship between food and the body.

Meanwhile the "marketeers" spin myths about physiological reasons you'll quickly shed excess belly fat by just popping pills and pooping their elixirs. People become confused between facts and fiction, and that often leads to dabbling rather than committing sweat and discipline. They reap dismal results. Meanwhile the stout folks among us rationalize lumping on an extra dollop of sour cream on a humungous potato while pondering why the scales continue to tip heavy.

Slight changes and modifications in a diet can be a good thing. Extreme changes can skew the body in another direction. Consider when we got the information that saturated fat (from animal products—meats, eggs, cheese) causes heart disease[6]. This finding motivated some to go vegan and eliminate all animal products. What many novices to the diet did was cut out the "sat fat" by limiting their diet to vegetables with polyunsaturated fats. Again research confuses more than it guides. A group recently concluded that low levels of sat fat in the body help the heart, and higher levels of polyunsaturated fats cause free radical damage that results in higher incidents of cancer.

---

6 http://www.naturalnews.com/035015_PUFAs_health_fatty_acids.html
For more information, visit http://www.tcolincampbell.org/plant-based-nutrition

What goes in must come out, and the only way to achieve this is to have a healthy digestive tract. Remember:

- Too much extra fat brings death too early a-knocking.

- A diet high in fiber keeps your colon healthy. What goes in should come out every day. Vegetables (raw is best), whole grains, and fruit are fiber-rich.

- Protein is good, lean protein is great. Fish and chicken provide the same nutritional value as beef and pork, but occasional beef and pork are okay.

- Fish (omega-3s) is great brain food. America's premier family physician, Dr. Bill Sears[7], says brains love omega-3s like bones love their calcium.

Valid and reliable reports are published in peer reviewed professional journals or clinical research studies. *The American Journal of Clinical Nutrition, Clinical Chemistry*, and the American Chemical Society, a Division of Agricultural and Food Chemistry have rigorous ways of determining the worth of research. Their audience is the scientific community rather than the general public. Few among us understand these highly technical articles. Be assured that the fitness industry knows there are not very many targeted consumers who are going to figure out the limitations of these studies.

A few years ago one of Karen's clients was excited about having found something on the internet which promised to build muscle. The product had been outlawed for distribution by the Food and Drug Administration (FDA). It did work, but the side effects far outweighed the benefits. The safety of a product is not guaranteed just because it claims to be "natural."

---

7 Bill Sears, William Sears, and Martha Sears, *Prime Time Health*. NY: Little Brown

Liberate Peace

Don't be deceived by shallow promises for quick fixes for problems that took a long time to develop. Siddhartha followed his own soul. He was most unhappy when he felt dragged through life by his desires—things others around him had and things he wanted but didn't really need. We become one with truth when we question the ways media exploits our wishes. Stay clear of the mad men who guarantee solutions to your problems. Instead, look inward and make peace with your own experience. Inner peace liberates us to move on through life in a wise and healthy way. Learn something new on every step in your path. Make love not war with food and your mind will make peace with your body.

> *"I arise in the morning torn*
> *between a desire to improve the world*
> *and a desire to enjoy the world.*
> *This makes it hard to enjoy the day."*
>
> *~ E.B. White*

*"Don't worry about
things you can't control.
It's enough to deal with the
things you can control."*

~ JAL

4

Relatively Speaking Fitness

Fitness Business

Fitness consultants are business people. Their goal is to earn a living. Some of them may help people to reach their wellness goals, but in many cases they stretch the truth about human physiology. They preach things that can, if believed, actually cause harm. What they don't admit to their clients is there is no fast and easy way to get in shape and lose weight. They might tell you their way is the easiest, best, fastest way but that is a marketing scheme.

One thing often left out of their spiel is that being thin does not guarantee good health. Not all slender people are in great shape. It's the same as thinking being rich means being happy. It doesn't always happen. No amount of money can make you truly happy, and no level of thinness will make you fit.

Karen got a letter from an 18-year-old girl who identified herself as a recovering anorexic. Her bodyweight was below 100 pounds. She was struggling to gain weight. Let's face it; what we eat is the key determinate of our health. She cried while she ate because of a gripping fear of food. She nearly ran herself to death by over-doing cardiovascular exercise. She moaned about the pain she felt while trying in vain to accept a healthy, athletic body image as "real". She craved the look of skinny magazine models. An irrational quest for thin almost cost her life.

The American public is so caught up on how people look that we've lost track of the more important question, *how do we feel?* It's certainly fine if you want to look better, and dropping 40 or more pounds makes you look more physically attractive. However, if weight loss comes at the expense of health then you haven't gone forward, you've stepped back. The human body is put together in a symbiotic way, which means each system depends on another to work correctly. When function is out of whack in one area, the domino effect takes over and dis-function and dis-ease reign. The human body is a miracle and a work of art. The only way to live a healthy and long life is to take care of it.

Feeling Fit

Shedding excess weight is a means toward living a longer, healthier life. Fitness is motivation made real. The fat around your body is a symptom of a myriad of physical and emotional problems. Think on a bigger scale by considering your whole body. Take this one step at a time. Say it with us, "To trim down, I have to raise up my fitness level!"

Early in her career Karen worked in a cardiac rehabilitation unit. Physicians sent their patients who had survived heart-related traumas. Compliant patients chose to act on the issue of their health. Some had learned the hard way that to ignore the basics of nutrition, exercise, and emotional wellbeing had nearly cost their lives. Their first move toward wellness was to eat a healthy, balanced diet as prescribed by their cardiologist.

They came into the exercise unit donned with tracking units accompanied by an exercise physiologist to monitor their heart functioning while they walked on a treadmill. The strength in their hearts and bodies returned slowly. The patients' physical and mental rehabilitation strategies were based on sound medicine. The sequence and pacing of exercises and the diets were geared toward predictable outcomes based on thousands of other patients with the same diagnosis. As they conditioned their hearts and lungs, while at the same time eating wisely, they lost weight.

Even patients with little extra fat on their bodies had terrific results. They became fit and healthier looking—inside and out. The positive results could be seen on the EKGs and in the mirrors. This isn't a great surprise. That's how the body works. Being physically fit and mentally committed to staying that way helped to ensure they wouldn't face another heart attack and not be so lucky. Choosing regular exercise, healthy eating habits, and maintaining a positive attitude meant they chose to live life to the fullest.

Fitness is a word thrown around in the exercise industry, but it's not given nearly the attention it deserves. It's seen as a nice aside to being thin and sexy. The industry's emphasis is on how people can make themselves look better. Have you ever known anyone who appeared to be in perfect physical condition when they died suddenly of a stroke or heart attack?

Looks are not the most optimal or accurate measure of one's health. Good looks won't make a difference if your heart and arteries are clogged. It is your responsibility to make yourself healthy. You matter to family, friends, work associates, and playmates. Be kind to them by caring for yourself.

We're not going to render medical advice other than to encourage readers to visit their doctors before embarking on any serious changes to their fitness lifestyle. Many health insurance policies cover wellness and prevention costs. These may include having a complete physical that usually includes blood work, an

EKG, a bone density test, and whatever else the doctor orders. Get ready for this important visit by making a list of your health history in your Journal. Be honest about your past and plans for the future. Explain to the doctor that you want to change your life by becoming fit. This is a vital step on your path to optimal personal fitness. You'll have a base level comparison for when your health reaches a level you never dreamed possible.

We opened this chapter discussing secrets of the fitness industry. The simple secrets of Zen involve breathing, smiling, and taking time to become increasingly aware of the world. Sometimes we become so focused on searching for answers to our problems that we miss finding the truth within.

Breathing Fitness

Take a moment to breathe in the world. Take a deep, deep breath through your nose and then slowly exhale, softly expelling air through your mouth. Go ahead and concentrate on breathing for the next 60 seconds. Shut your eyes and breathe.

Think about breathing. Visualize how the unconscious nervous system coordinated the actions of many body parts in order to breathe. The diaphragm contracted downward to make space for the lungs to expand. As they expanded, air was sucked down the windpipe and into the lungs. Next, the air passed through tiny bronchial tubes, raced into air sacs then slipped into blood capillaries that took it to the heart and was then pumped through the body. The first secret of Zen is, just breathe. Bring into your body that which provides for optimal life. Conversely, blow out the bad. Exhale the negative thoughts and wastes that serve as potholes on your pathway to fitness.

Grins Win

The second Zen secret is to smile. Our facial features express our understanding of the world, of all that we breathe in, and the freedom gained by exhaling all we don't need. Again, we can search for ways to become fit, but we have to find what we already know from past experiences about fitness and health. Knowing what is good within and what opportunities abound in the world come from living in harmony with the world around us. Smiling shows that we get what we've got.

Smiles are often described as being bright. This is all part of Zen. Being bright is a symbol of enlightenment that is achieved by having a balance between the good within and the goodness of life. Breathe deeply and smile. Feels good, doesn't it?

Laughter is good medicine, according to Daniel Amen, M.D.[8] A good laugh bolsters the immune system and lowers toxic stress hormones. Laughing gives the mind-body a swift jolt of endorphins.

Timing Fitness

Take time to make time. Einstein's theory of relativity included his conclusion that time travel is possible. He described time as a rubber band. It's elastic with no beginning or end. To move very, very fast, in fact to even attempt to move faster than light would make one extremely heavy, and would stop actual movement. Think of it as moving so fast you become too dense to move any more. Or, think of it as trying fad diets, taking dangerous herbal substances, or over exercising.

The result? At first you seem to rapidly reach your goal of losing weight, but for some odd reason you start to flow backwards to that uncomfortable body form that started the journey. That's

---

8 Daniel G. Amen, M.D. (2010). *Change Your Brain Change Your Body.* NY: Harmony Books

Einstein's science—you traveled forward all the way back to where you started. Is it destiny or density? You were too dense, er, dumb, to sense that you were going nowhere near your goal.

Change takes time. The simple law of physics is that if matter moves too fast, it becomes so heavy and dense that it simply implodes on itself and becomes a black hole. That which goes too fast in too short of time simply ceases to be part of this universe.

Breathe deep, smile, and take your time. If you want to become fit, keep focused on exactly where you are now in terms of reaching this goal. Believe you can be fit, work toward making your dreams the truth of your life and you will one day awaken healthy and fit. It's what we call the Now and Zen of weight loss.

> *"Smile, breathe, and go slowly."*
>
> *~ Thich Nhat Hanh*

> *"Grin and go."*
>
> *~ JAL*

5

Quick Kills Slowly

Hazards

There are obstacles to healthy living lurking next to the register at the checkout counter of grocery stores and quick shops. Crunchies! Sweet and salty treats! Gobs of sugary goo to woo you! These sources of trouble are stealthily placed to snag customers' attentions and raid their wallets. Junk foods don't carry hazard warnings that say, "This pretty wrapping disguises a trap to keep eaters from becoming thin." Escaping from a world that enabled you to gain too much weight is not easy or impossible.

Start the trek to an ideal weight by avoiding two powerful hazards, junk food and fast food. Ban them from your daily routine. Snack companies saturate the marketplace with junk food. Michael Pollan[9] describes much of what sits on grocery shelves as "edible food-like substances." One of the best marketing strategies is to hook children early. School children who eat food from vending

---

9 Michael Pollan, Professor of science and environmental journalism at UC Berkeley. His book, *The Omnivore's Dilemma: A Natural History of Four Meals*, was named one of the ten best books of 2006 by the *New York Times* and the *Washington Post*.

machines are more likely to develop poor eating habits. Grabbing a candy bar or salty snack everyday easily leads to becoming overweight, obese, or at risk for chronic health problems such as diabetes and coronary artery disease. These conclusions were drawn from research done at University of Michigan Medical School which isn't trying to sell anything—it's trying to understand how early eating habits affect health later in life.

There is a growing resistance to being lured into a lifetime of craving food that kills. Kids who grow up in low-income neighborhoods are really vulnerable. Why? Fast food is a lot of cheap food. What do we call drive-thru serving sizes? Super! Better yet, kids can get free stuff with their super-sized high caloric meals. Well, not everywhere. San Francisco passed an ordinance that forbids restaurants from hooking kids on food that may harm their health by giving away toys with meals that are loaded with calories, fat, and sugar. The backers of this agenda call it a step towards "food justice."

Drive-through restaurants offer "value meals", cheap food with lots of salt, fat, and sugar. Fans cite two bonus points for those in a hurry to grab, gulp, and go. The food can be chowed down fast in the comfort of the front seat of a car and fast food can be found any time of day. For those domesticated few that choose to eat at home—quickly with no fuss or muss, there's the frozen food grocery or quick shop aisles solidly stocked with microwavable meals.

Oddly enough, the American public consumes processed and purified food never intended for human consumption. A diet based on processed, chemically enhanced, genetically manipulated food does not bode well for a long and healthy life span. Why poison yourself? Does feeling poorly make you feel better? Bad food isn't good enough for you! The truth is food chains don't care what is best for their customers. They care about their bottom profit line while you care about your bottom size. The conflict is between corporate wealth and personal health.

Change is a chain of events that allows us to pass from one state to another. Slide from here to there by browsing a few web pages about the grease in fast food. Did you know it's recycled into car fuel and dog food? Visit the National Institute of Health[10] web site and learn more about nutrition.

Not long ago, a chicken franchise tried to run an advertising campaign showing people excited about the "healthy" food they were eating for dinner. The camera zoomed in on a container stuffed with deep fried, breaded chicken. Does this sort of marketing meet truth in advertising standards? It deliberately misleads people to believe that chicken fried in trans fats and loaded with sodium is a healthy choice. It's not.

Sure, fried food tastes good, but is a few mouthfuls and a greasy chin worth around 500 calories and 30 grams of fat? Fried chicken isn't toxic but it's not by any means good for our bodies. Pulling the skin off exposes the meat that has been immersed and saturated with grease. Chicken already has a lot of fat, so fried chicken is fat made fatter. Not that it seems to matter to people hooked on fried chicken. There's an urban legend of a chicken franchise owner who grumbled that an internal survey of over 600 stores showed that half of all the healthier grilled chicken doesn't sell so it's thrown away every day.

Adults, like children, aren't designed to handle chemicals in the form of seasonings and colors. Hundreds of chemicals are in foods served in school cafeterias and at kitchen tables. Unfortunately, short of growing, picking, and eating your own, becoming what's called a *locavore*, it is hard to avoid them.

Synthetic *adj.*: fake, mock, unreal

Many edibles have something in common—they contain synthetic materials. The natural food, whether plant or animal, is altered by a chemical process. They are not natural to the body and consequently are often not tolerated well in great quantities over time. Love those freakish blazing red Maraschino cherries? Do you think that's the color of freshly picked cherries? Last year the European Parliament acted on recent findings on synthetic food colors and hyperactivity. Now across Europe, products containing synthetic food colors carry warning labels stating, "consumption may have an adverse effect on activity and attention in children." So much for blue popsicles.

People respond differently to food additives. Rashes, acne, weight gain, and food allergies are among the bad reactions. There appear to be growing numbers of young people with life threatening food allergies. The most frightening thing about additives is that they aren't thoroughly tested, especially not in combination. We should reconsider feeding kids chemical stews with no idea how their bodies will be affected over time.

Apparently, our bodies set some of these toxic chemicals aside to deal with another day. Think of this as the *Scarlet O'Hara Effect*; Deal with your problems later. In the meantime these chemicals rest against a comfy pancreas, liver, or breast tissue. Some chemicals offer a spa treatment that vitalizes cancer cells.

Control

Eating is out of control on a national level. Obesity is now regarded as a *chronic disease*. Health and fitness are no longer issues of fitting into a smaller size or looking forever young; they represent a struggle to survive. In 2003, the Zambian government refused humanitarian aide for its starving nation.[11] It would not allow genetically modified (GM) grain sent from the United States to cross its borders. The media reported, "President Mwanawasa pleaded with Zambians to be "patient" while the government does all it can to secure non-GM food. 'I will not allow Zambians to be turned into guinea pigs no matter the levels of hunger in the country.'"

So, what are we Americans eating if our amber grains are too toxic for starving Zambians? We are eating food produced by our farmers grown from genetically modified seeds. Our nation's largest seed company has a global marketplace. We have little recourse as they hold a monopoly on seed production and release only GM seeds. Don't think you are protected by the government because you aren't. They offer this food as gifts to those suffering famine.[12]

The truth is we all invite many dangerous substances into our bodies at one time or another. Even too much pure mountain spring water can have detrimental effects. Next we face long-term illness where we struggle with one ailment after another. It's our worst nightmare filled with hours at the doctor's office and thousands of dollars in medicine. That isn't living well.

We are what we eat. We'd like to look fresh rather than wilted, lean—not marbled with fat. We prefer to be a body that's clean not cluttered with additives and known by our names not by our ingredients. Looking fit and being healthy in part comes from our choices as to what grown products we choose to eat.

Less Isn't Nothing

Another barrier between fitness and illness is not eating enough food. Brains struggle to cope with mixed messages. Some people get busy and forget to eat. Others feel that less is more. It isn't. Deprive a body of food and it shuts down its energy burning functions. Sensors trip into survival mode. The body starts hoarding

12 For more information go to www.organicconsumers.org

fat, water, and calories. These are the very things a dieter hopes to lose!

A food-deprived body slows its metabolism. This is ironic. People stop eating to speed up a diet! This is not a rational choice. Remember Einstein's theory? Any matter that moves too fast eventually slows down and in the long run is right where it began. A slow metabolism doesn't burn much of anything but time. One way to trick the brain into letting loose with its hoarding habit is to kick in some exercise and boost the metabolism.

A car without gas doesn't move. Hunger pangs are a body's low fuel light just like on a car's dashboard. Like a car, your body is not very reliable when the lights go off warning that you're running on empty. Driving down the road with shaking hands because your body's re-routing energy to essential organs critical to life isn't wise. Cars and people aren't built to run on fumes.

Fall Awake

Healthy snacks fuel life-sustaining chemical activity. Raw almonds are a great snack. They fit nicely in glove boxes, brief cases, and pockets. Besides being compact and portable, almonds are low fat and high protein. They're naturally packed with enough carbohydrates to keep your internal engine humming for an hour or two until it is time to eat.

Feel Your Pain

Our loves become ever more meaningful, moment-to-moment because our emotions help our minds. Emotions allow us to know our limits and reach for the sky. You don't need to apologize for lusting for a trim body. Rather than pretend not to care about how you look and feel, learn to deal with these feelings as attachments.

Part of the Zen of eating well is to relate to these attachments without clinging, acting out, or trying to hide them deeper in your mind. In this way, by letting go of negative feelings and a weak self-image, you become free and can choose how to respond.[13]

Gifting

This chapter is about awakening your mind to see foods as either compatible or not with your inner vision of how you want to look and feel. Think about how body is fueled and whether or not it repays you in terms of feeling good and being healthy. Becoming grossly overweight and physically weak is the body's opposition to mindless eating habits.

Learn to see food as gifts your mind gives to its body to symbolize their love for each other. Rather than rush through a quick bite relish every morsel that goes into your mouth. Slow down and savor what you eat. Look at what's on your plate. Consider its shape and color. Notice the way it is arranged. Let fresh vegetables seduce your taste buds. Breathe in the sultry scents of herbs and spices that enhance simple flavors. Become aware of emotions that arise from food aromas. Concentrate on the complex tastes of different food textures. What words come to mind? What memories do the sights of a delicious and nutritious meal invoke? Write about these in your journal. Don't be surprised or ashamed if your description of a slowly savored meal reads like a paperback bodice ripper!

Imagine food as the mind's gift chosen to energize, soothe, comfort, and nurture its body. Your grateful body will respond to these gifts by controlling its urges for more than it needs. It will stop hording fat and water as it becomes lighter of being and easier

---

13 See R. Kabat Snick, (1998), *The Zen of Eating: Ancient Answers to Modern Wight Problems.* CA: San Francisco: The Berkley Publishing Group.

to move. When you protect your body from harm, given time, it changes in ways that make it appear more like the pleasing form drawn in your mind's eye. You've got to let it go and let it be.

"Learn to recognize the counterfeit coins that may buy you just a moment of pleasure, then drag you for days like a broken man behind a farting camel."

~ Hafiz of Persia

"I guess it took a long time to make me. I've got to make time to change me."

~ JAL

6

Organic or NOT: Minding Peas and Qs

Many folks would be hard pressed to explain the difference between organic and conventionally produced food. Let's try to answer a few questions about organic food. What is it? Is it safer to eat than regular food? Is it better nutritionally? Does it taste good? Is an organic diet economically feasible on your budget? After reading this chapter you can decide whether it's worth the time, effort, and expense to "go green." For starters, don't buy something just because it's labeled organic—remember the pitfalls of marketing to the uninformed masses! Let's build your knowledge about differences between organic and conventional food before going grocery shopping.

Coming to Terms

The word organic refers to the way farmers grow and process food. Food covers a broad range of things to eat, from vegetables and grains to fish and meat. According to experts at the Mayo Clinic (they are physicians not farmers) organic farmers plant and harvest in ways that preserve and conserve soil and water[14]. In order not to pollute the land, sea, and air they use unconventional methods to fertilize crops, prevent livestock disease, as well as to control weeds and pests. Conventional farming uses chemicals to promote plant growth while organic farming involves natural fertilizers such as manure and compost (decayed plant matter).

In an ideal world we would eat organic foods grown and harvested by our grandparents. Let's be real. They probably sold their home with the little patch of garden out back and moved down to Florida to sit out the winters. Not to worry, we have more resources available to us today than even five years ago.

Be cautious of organic foods. The United States Department of Agriculture Organic (USDA) has government standards for foods to be labeled organic.[15] Only products certified 95 percent or more are allowed to display the organic USDA sticker. There are organic levels:

- **100 percent organic.** Products completely organic or made of all organic ingredients.

- **Organic.** Products that are at least 95 percent organic.

- **Made with organic ingredients.** These are products that contain at least *70 percent organic* ingredients. The organic seal can't be used on these packages.

- Foods containing *less than 70% organic* ingredients can only use the word organic on it.

The hitch comes in the fact that merchants can use other labels like "free-range", "all-natural" or "hormone-free" but these don't necessarily mean the food was produced pesticide and chemical free. They are not organic.

---

14 http://www.mayoclinic.com/health/organic-food/NU00255

15 Organic Certification | USDA - US Department of Agriculture www.usda.gov/wps/portal/usda/usdahome?navid=ORGANIC

The answer to the question is organic food safer to eat than conventional food? It depends. If we go back to the Hippie mantra of the '60s, "you are what you eat" choosing between organic and conventional is a toss up for many people who feel that eating pesticides is about as appealing as eating cow manure.

Then again, pesticides are designed to kill while healthy animals process naturally what they eat. If they don't eat killer chemicals we can assume their output is relatively benign.

Farm animals that are not fed a diet supplemented with hormones, antibiotics, and other chemical growth-promoting cocktails produce organic fertilizer. Organically raised cows produce milk enriched with more healthy vitamins, antioxidants, and healthy fat than milk produced conventionally. There aren't enough studies that actually compare all organic foods with conventional counterparts. A rutabaga by any name or farming technique may be just another rutabaga.

Oh! The Cost of Green!

Is organic food affordable on your budget? It is more expensive than conventional food because it costs more to produce. Organic farming is hands on. Farmers produce less food than giant agribusinesses and since there is less it costs more. A common complaint echoed by media pundits is that wealthy agriculture conglomerates feed the poor while poor organic farmers feed the rich.

Green Ink

Let's get back to the food journal. An example of some questions you might ask yourself and a suggested format can be found in the Appendix. We're not suggesting you change your diet yet. Everybody needs to discover his or her own personal comfort level.

You'll want to try a few organic foods and determine whether they are worth the extra cost. It is unrealistic to think anyone makes changes until clearly understanding the complex relationship between food and the human body.

List the food you eat. Next, describe how you feel after you eat. Be sure to note changes in mood and energy level. Pay attention to even the slightest gastric changes. Even sinus congestion can be the effect of a mismatch between certain foods and your body.

We are affected by food all the time. Take Thanksgiving dinner for example. Ever notice how everyone nods off after that big dinner? Everybody blames it on the turkey. Ever think that in addition to the tryptophan (an amino acid that acts like a sedative) in the turkey their bodies are responding to other things they ate? And, by the way, it takes a big dose of tryptophan on an *empty* stomach to trick the brain into thinking its time for a nap. Make a list of all the traditional side dishes and desserts served at Thanksgiving. The nod-off could be a reaction any item in combination with mashed potatoes, green bean casserole, stuffing, corn, candied yams, cranberry sauce, rolls, and pie.

In just one Thanksgiving meal the typical American consumes more carbohydrates and sugar than an athlete does in a month. Holiday over-eating makes the pancreas work overtime pumping out insulin to deal with the elevated levels of blood glucose (sugar). When someone's pancreas wears out, a person becomes a patient with diabetes.

Food is Fuel

Following the last chapter about fueling your body, let's think about the breakdown that lies ahead. Food is digested or broken down so it can be used as energy. In order to make energy, sugar (glucose) has to break into the blood stream. The pancreas has to stay busy producing insulin so that the energy created by the glucose can get to the engine parts; the muscle, fat, and liver where it's used as fuel. People with diabetes have an uncontrolled surplus of sugar in their blood that never is converted to fuel. The system backfires and health complications develop that are serious threats to life.

Readers of this book are interested in establishing a comfortable fitness level. Many readers are probably tossing around the conundrum, why can't I just have a smaller pant size and a flatter abdomen but skip the fitness gig? Fitness is what's going to keep you in that ideal pant size without the pooch beyond the first few months of weight loss. You don't want to have as many diet honeymoons as Liz Taylor had wedding nights.

Optimal Living

Living at an optimal fitness level is dependent on being able to live with you. We're getting close to a psychotherapist's spin on lifestyle choices and their consequences because changes in activity and eating are profound. People seem to be rarely satisfied with what they have and who they are. Those issues involve self-esteem and image. We're not qualified to approach that subject, but there are plenty of places to go for help. Just remember Sheryl Crow's advice, "It's not what you need. It's that you get what you got."

We *are* qualified to help you get rolling on an exercise and eating program. How much you change and whether you achieve and maintain your fitness goals gets kick started by paying attention to your body and writing a food journal.

Eating mindfully is about consuming fresh and lean food in moderation. Good taste is not exclusive to gravy, sauces, and cheese. Enhance simple foods with a variety of herbs and spices many of which have more disease fighting antioxidants than fruits and vegetables. Introduce your palate to new tastes and learn to appreciate how food flavors are enhanced. Many herbs can be grown in small pots right in the kitchen.

David Simon, M.D., makes eating well a simple thing.[16] He recommends a diet that provides all six tastes at every meal. Fill your grocery cart with foods that taste salty, sweet, sour, pungent, bitter, and stringent. In your journal make a list of your personal favorites in each category. Create meals that are balanced, fresh, and absolutely delicious. Healthy choices from a broad array of selection will promote wellbeing and decrease stress.

Drink water, and eat your vegetables and fruit. And by the way, eating fruit is better than drinking fruit. That is because most fruit juices are supplemented with sugar and other additives. We all know many ways to fitness but few actually walk the talk. Add to the list whole grains and lean meats and you are well on your way to good health. Be mindful of what you eat. Relax while you eat. Simply take it in.

Do you eat to live or live to eat? Eating is not just a means of fueling your engine. Done right, eating healthy is truly one of the great joys of living.

"We have more possibilities available at the moment than we realize."

~ Thitch Nhat Hanh

"I don't know. I think. I get it."

~ JAL

16 Simon M.D., David. *The Chopra Center Herbal Handbook*, New York. Three Rivers Press. 2000

Mind-full-ness

7

Most journeys end where they begin. The traveler returns home. When embarking on a long road trip, it's common to make sure the car is tuned up, the tires rotated and oil changed. We approach fitness from the stance that its essential to get our minds tuned up and become optimally aware of the present. The future and the past are powerful concepts that too often separate our attention from the moment in hand.

Unlike an impatient child in the back seat asking, "are we there yet?" mindfulness is the sense that wherever we are is "there now." We are mindful when our complete attention is focused on the experience of the present—it is a mind-expanding gift. It allows each person to give up anything else except what is happening at a given moment in time.

Mindfulness is clear comprehension that is non-judgmental. It is a concentration of mind and body that accompanies a keen and calm awareness of our bodily functions, feelings, thoughts and perception, and consciousness. The grand adventure of mindfulness is exploring who you are and where you are. Right here, right now.

Foster Thinking Clearly

Mindfulness is a universal human capacity to foster clear thinking. It infuses one's perceptions about life with acute awareness of the present. Mindfulness is understanding and being grateful for now. Mindfulness is not associated with any particular religions or cultures though it was long associated with Eastern philosophies. Today mindfulness institutes are housed in medical schools and multinational corporations. Clinical research has show that mindfulness is an effective way to treat a host of mental and physical ailments such as anxiety, depression, and disordered eating.[17]

Meditation is a pathway to mindfulness. Meditation cultivates awareness of the present moment. It is a way to relate directly to whatever is happening in your life at a given moment in time. It is a way to take charge of that moment by doing something no one else can do to be one in spirit, mind, and body. Researchers at the University of Massachusetts Medical School teach patients though meditation exercises to work consciously and systematically to deal with their stress, pain, illness, challenges, and demands of everyday life.[18] They learn to make friends with their minds and use mind-body allies so they can better deal with their lot in life.

Formal meditation exercises can be as "simple" as learning to surf your breathing. Exercising the mind is as important as mounting the elliptical—it is wakefulness to life. Deepak Chopra says that meditation is a way to know our inner intelligence.[19] He's referring to the part of our mind that is not limited to the brain but is a consciousness that mirrors the wisdom of the universe.

---

17 See Mindfulness in Medicine. Lugwig & Zinn. Available online at http://jama.ama-assn.org/cgi/content/short/300/11/1350

18 See Center for Mindfulness. Available online at http://umassmed.edu/cfm/stress/index.aspx

19 See www.chopra.com/meditation

Feeling the Now

Mindfulness helps us to live as if it really matters. And it does—for you and yours in more ways than we can imagine. By meditating, one is not self-medicating to blot out feelings and thoughts. It is a way to let you work your way through your mind. Meditation involves an awareness of the relationship to our inner-self, nature, and others that is boundless and infinitely available at any moment. It begins when we let go of wanting to be or do anything else but what is happening now. It is the union of being and doing that takes place within. This awakens an attitude of gratitude for the everyday stuff of life. This isn't necessarily a great *aha* moment as much as it is a peacefulness that comes from focusing on now.

The human mind is a busy place. It hosts 60,000 to 80,000 thoughts a day. The mind exists beyond the brain and at any given moment random thoughts compete for attention. Dr. Candace Pert, a neuroscientist inferred from her study of peptides (chemicals) and the brain, that emotions create the communication network between our minds and bodies.[20] Gut feelings, butterflies in our stomachs, and stress headaches are often triggered by our emotional reactions to events. With meditation we don't strive to quiet the communication, rather we accept that we often don't know why we feel or act in a certain way.

Meditation allows us to mentally step aside from our information network and emotions to allow our minds to take in the sensations it is receiving at that moment. We become sensitive, or aware, of what we hear within our consciousness as well as through our ears. Each has powerful input into our perception of what is real. Consciousness is a "mind-body" experience.

An initial meditation exercise is to concentrate on the unconscious act of breathing. This doesn't mean you have to stop breathing in order to meditate—your lungs do the job using

---

20 See www.candacepert.com or read her book, *The Molecules of Emotions*, 1998

part of the brain that doesn't need to check in with its hub of consciousness. Begin by arranging yourself in a comfortable way that reflects your dignity. You can close your eyes, stare at the wall, contemplate your navel, or gaze at a full screen meditation video on YouTube or at the Chopra Center's web page.[21]

Take a deep breath through your nose. Let your diaphragm release its tension on the lungs. You may choose a mantra, a "mind vehicle" such as the word "Om" on which to focus. Breathe in and release the breath through your mouth. Give up your wants and needs. Just focus on the air escaping. One breath at a time. Now. Just ride the air and be free.

It's unlikely that you'll be able to quiet your sense of "I" as you learn to meditate. While mindfulness is about relating directly to whatever is happening in your life it doesn't need verbalization. The mind knows the world in many ways through its senses that by passes our language center of the brain. Learn to navigate these exciting pathways without subvocalizing (talking in the head) a commentary about the perceptions of this experience.

"Gratitude is one of the sweet shortcuts to finding peace of mind and happiness inside. No matter what is going on outside of us, there's always something we could be grateful for."

~ Barry Neil Kaufman

"So, this is smiling with my liver. Yes.
It's the purifying of my experiences
of the moment throughout my mind,
body, and spirit. The bile of a grin it is."

~ JAL

8

Zen the Next Gen

Dr. Jon Kabat-Zinn[22] at the University of Massachusetts School of medicine, himself a dad, observed that being a parent is one of the greatest mindfulness practices of all. Illness and death play important roles in life. Living life to its fullest involves knowing that time passes ever more swiftly when we make choices that squander opportunities for wellness. Children need role models who demonstrate living healthy and prospering rather than living riskily and floundering.

Research often articulates the obvious. People who cycle through repeated weight gains and losses find it harder and harder to maintain a healthy weight. One study concludes that formerly overweight people eventually need to eat 15% fewer calories than people who are thin and maintain the same weight.[23] This means that young children who are exposed to healthy diets and encouraged to run around and play have a greater chance of not becoming overweight adults.

---

22 See www.youtube.com/watch?v=fEINtdXIqns
23 http://www.drsharma.ca/obesitywhy-is-it-so-hard-to-maintain-a-reduced-body-weight.html

One of the best gifts parents can give their kids is to feed them a healthy diet. Our adult eating patterns are the effects of two things parents pass on to their kids, their genes and eating habits. The eating habits young kids develop last a lifetime.

Rational people don't walk across the street on red in the midst of rush hour traffic. Public safety measures include crosswalks, and flashing lights with timers on every city street corner to jolt pedestrians' attention. This guide is something like a crossing guard—the goal is to achieve fitness in a safe and lasting way.

Science of Hope

Human DNA involves more than inheriting family traits like eye color or risk for certain diseases. Parents' behaviors can also be passed on to the next generation. Being overweight, abusing drugs, and smoking are behavioral traits that may actually change an adult's DNA that in turn is inherited by their babies. Researchers are also discovering the extent to which pharmaceuticals, pesticides, air pollutants, industrial chemicals, hormones, and nutrition can change people's genetic makeup passed on to subsequent generations.

This is the science of hope. If chemical modifications to DNA may affect the activity of key genes involved in regulating body weight, it raises the possibility that scientists could discover environmental factors beyond calorie intake and exercise that influence body size.

Next Zen-eration

Eating is essential for life. Kids need to learn what foods are best for them. Orange Jell-O is not a fruit. A recent survey of over 900 kids asked them how many vegetables they ate yesterday.[24] A quarter of

24 http://www.news.com.au/diet-of-junk-food-for-wa-kids/story-e6frg13u-1226155146900

the kids had three or more and a third had none. Kids learn early to eat what they're given. At age one, Jeri's granddaughter's favorite foods were broccoli and avocados. She's growing up green! Given daily opportunities to consume a balanced diet, kids will develop healthy eating habits. It's up to their caretakers to provide them with the right fuel to keep their bodies in motion and healthy.

Parents can pass healthy habits on to their children. Choosing routines that keep the family active may reap healthy descendants for generations to come.

Kids need to develop the habit of moving their bodies from one place to the next at different rates of speed. Running, skipping, hopping, pushing, lifting, and pulling are the natural movements of childhood. Many school budgets have cut the requirements for physical education. A typical punishment for being too lazy to finish homework is to miss recess. Kids get to sit around and do nothing rather than run around and play. Students get in trouble for running in the halls and moving around unnecessarily in their classrooms. It's up to parents to show them movement and exercise as part of the family's lifestyle.

Find a comfortable approach to healthy eating. Try to clean with healthy products and avoid packaged and processed foods. Pack light snacks for the kids to eat while running errands and bypass the drive-thru.

If your purpose in life is to be a beloved parent, nurture your children and build relationships. Live to see your children well into adulthood—they need you. You'll need the energy to go to their games and cheer from the sidelines, or better yet, coach the team! Your body must be able to withstand late nights tending to sick children, early morning swim practice carpools, endless laundry, and if you're lucky, chasing your grandkids. We all are called to teach the next generation how to care for themselves. If you want your children to be healthy, simply model good choices that give them a variety of healthy fuels for good energy, clear thinking, and a centered spirit.

Build a healthy lifestyle. Lessen your attachment to foods of convenience. Make time to shop at the local farmers market and reduce your food's carbon footprint. Avoid the foods found in the middle of the grocery store. A pantry full of canned vegetables and boxes of dried provisions is a throw back to the dawn of the nuclear age when people feared a third world war and prepared to avoid the fall out by hiding in their bunkers.

Choose

This chapter began with dark hints that some illness and to a certain extent, at least for a while, death, can be avoided or activated by our choices. A healthy environment, regular activity and motion, and healthy fuel are ways to avoid bad stuff. It's said that kids are natural Zen masters because they see the world as brand new place and their focus is on living for the moment. Giving kids ample opportunities to grow up happy, healthy, and wise starts with wising up to the things that make ourselves happiest and healthiest so that we literally pass it on.

"If you want happiness for a lifetime—help the next generation."

~ Chinese Proverb

"You are my sunshine."

~ JAL

Weight

"If you cannot find the truth right where you are, where else do you expect to find it?"

~ Chuang-tzu

Motivation + Practice = Success

After about three weeks into the ZWL you'll behave as one who's committed. Keep moving toward success. Bravo! Take a look in the mirror and at your journal. The effects of your mindful approach to ZWL are ever more positive mental, emotional and physical states of being. ZWL results are directly proportionate to each person's level of effort. Effort is driving your success. You're the prime beneficiary of this hard slog toward fitness and wellness. In a word, you're motivated. That you can attribute this success to your effort means that the motivation energizing your steadfastness is intrinsic—it comes from within. You soar with the self-knowledge and acclamation that, "I can do and I do."

Self-Determined Success

Your success is *self-determined*—it's the result of being proactive and engaged rather than alienated and passive about your personal wellbeing. Your personal health plan is working!

Let's take a moment to think about motivation and *why* you are learning to master and enhance this energy. One of the positive potentials of being human is the inherent need to seek out novelty and challenge. People strive to extend and exercise their capacities to explore and learn. Psychologists have long asserted that healthy people are active, inquisitive, curious, and playful. Why? These constructs bring about pure pleasure. They are essential for healthy minds and positive social development. We're driven to engage with the world and by doing so we can become better or worse for the experience.

Arouse the Flow

Why is motivation key to good versus bad lifestyle? Let's begin with the sense of drive—it's an internal force that pushes people to be effective within their environment. It's the inner drive that gets you walking the dogs on a blustery spring morning, mounting the elliptical, clapping to the music's beat during a group workout. When people feel competent they sense heightened self-confidence and their self-esteem increases. At the same time, this drive clicks when in certain environments such as sailing on a clear sea. Part of the ZWL program is figuring out where and when you sense this *optimal stimulation.*

The ZWL is a way to optimally arouse your energy to eat right and move a lot. Your interest and energy are focused. Sustaining this focus is a challenge best met by assuring that you maintain contact with people, activities, and routines that stimulate and arouse your motivation. Perhaps it's time to fine-tune your ZWL program from a motivational perspective.

Let's say you're jogging down a nature trail and come toe to fang with a great big snake. My level of arousal would go way beyond optimal. I'd "freak out," probably lose my footing and collide with the snake. If my level of arousal was not so high, my brain would quickly command a U turn and I'd flee the trail. This would lower my arousal and give my head a "good job" pat of reinforcement. This sense of success will motivate any future encounters with snakes; I'll instantly high tail out of there.

On the other hand, the next time I visit the zoo I might find myself drawn to a big thick snake safely behind the exhibit glass. Why would I be drawn to a creature that terrifies me? It is because there is still a trace of the sense of arousal left in my brain from that scary encounter with the snake in the wild.

Why does this explanation of motivation and optimal arousal help us understand the effects of a particular weight loss and fitness program? Because the "taste of excitement" experienced as you become stronger, leaner, and joyful will not be entirely forgotten. In fact, the more these sensations are reinforced, the more your mind and body crave them. This means the threat associated with a hard work out (This is going to hurt tomorrow!) and the puzzle of making the program work actually impel you to achieve and maintain success. You're hooked on fitness!

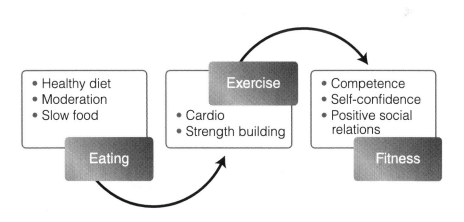

Personal Control

Motivation is also affected by one's personal sense of control. It's healthier to an extent to believe we have control over things we are able to influence. This is known as internal control. We all become more in tuned with our inner power as we grow older. This is one of the many benefits of chronological enhancement!

Sources of control and motivation

Internal Locus of Control	External Locus of Control
Behavior is controlled by personal abilities, decisions, and efforts	Behavior is controlled by fate or luck and other external factors

On the flip side, too much internal control isn't healthy. People can become neurotic and anxious by being overly concerned about their competencies in light of certain, difficult responsibilities. Control is by and large something within a realm of the competencies one has, and their personal beliefs during opportunities to make a decisions.

Sometimes, it's wise to take an external perspective by acknowledging a difficult task is outside, such as the rotten luck of encountering sleet midway through a brisk walk in the park. You decide that rather than to push ahead and risk slipping on ice, you'll turn home for a simmering cup of hot tea.

Learning a new strategy that's designed to make something specific happen is one thing—fully integrating that strategy into daily routines is much more difficult. It's estimated that teachers need to practice a new technique at least 15 times before it becomes an automatic skill. It becomes part of routine that makes a real difference in what happens next. Patients who are diagnosed with rare and complicated illnesses are often referred to a physician with the extensive experience providing specific treatments. We are talking about the effects of practice.

Rewards

The outcomes of practice let us know if we are making progress and approaching success. For some people, a perfect performance is its own reward. The joy is within the sense of doing something well. At other times, the payoff may be an external award. Rewards are integral to many self help and rehab programs; key fobs for being clean and sober, stickers for losing five pounds, and certificates of accomplishment are all external rewards. There is a dark side to rewards. Sometimes what was once a satisfying thing to do becomes motivated by an external source of control.

Here's an example.

A friend of ours during her first months of marriage experienced pure delight by keeping her new home sparkling clean and serving her husband delicious gourmet dinners even after they both survived hectic workdays. One evening she found a $100 bill tucked under her napkin when they sat down for dinner.

"What's this for?" she asked her husband.

"Honey, all the other guys complain that their house is a mess and they eat slop or fast food for dinner. They're miserable. I figure we save so much money not having a cleaning service or eating out so much I should give you a little reward for your hard work!"

She was surprised and yet pleased. Over the next couple of weeks she continued to clean and cook, but caught herself peaking beneath the napkin for another "reward".

One night the husband returned home and was confused. No delicious aroma of dinner greeted him. Oddly enough, there were dirty breakfast dishes on the kitchen counter. His tighty whities were right on the bathroom floor where he'd dropped them and the table was unset. A bit disoriented he asked, "Honey, what did you make for dinner?"

"Reservations", she curtly replied.

The hidden cost of external rewards for our newlyweds was the change from doing something for the intrinsic pleasure associated with "doing just that" to doing something, and then expecting the greater pleasure is begotten from an external reward. The value of the action is trumped.

Locus of Control

How we view the locus for control in the Zen Weight Loss program varies from level to level as well as season to season. By weighing the potential for an extra workout to balance a special dinner occasion you're assessing your personal ability to invest extra effort to achieve a reward. Deciding that the odds are stacked against you with too many temptations to eat fast, move slow, or just sit back and see what happens in a no fly zone. It's time to revisit your journal and recall the moments of optimal arousal and optimal engagement that reflect your quest for fitness. What makes your socks roll up and down?

The Zen of Weight Loss is essentially a process where proponents learn to manage their sense of control over lifestyle and wellbeing. Unlike the majority of Americans who don't exercise regularly, you choose to improve your health. You have chosen to balance your will with fate and your effort with life's difficulties. You seek and find optimal opportunities to sustain your focus and energy on wellness and wellbeing.

Karen's Koans

Let's talk about pain. There are three kinds of pain you might experience. The first is the muscle fatigue you can experience during exercise—when you don't think you can pull that cord one more time. This is normal. The second is DOMS (Delayed Onset Muscle Soreness). This soreness is felt within two days of starting a new workout or when a workout is changed. This discomfort goes away in a few days. These pains are part of exercise but DOMS can be avoided by being reasonable with the demands made on your body. Easy does it! The pain to avoid is the sudden sharp pain resulting from an injury. This is tactile proof that you have overdone it. This pain can send you to the doctor. Be smart and take it easy.

"Emotions last for seconds.
Moods last for a day.
Temperament is forged over years."

~ *Matthieu Ricard*
(in Destructive Emotions)

"I feel good about this.
Then again, I didn't
feel bad about that."

~ JAL

10

Choose Fitness That Fits

Two things to understand before you go any further with your body restoration. First, you gave yourself permission to take charge of your fitness and diet routine, and second, you never get a day off. You'd miss it!

Come to grips with what you want. If you don't want to lug around love handles then decide where you want to be on the fitness scale; a loafer, someone comfortable in their own skin, or a full blown fitness fanatic. Think about the consequences of trying to maintain your chosen level of fitness. Let's look at three fitness prototypes, the loafer, the optimal, and the fanatic.

Loafers

Obviously if you're reading this book you want to make changes and be happier at a more trim and fit level. If you're at Fitness Level #1, the *Loafer* level, think about its current status. Here are some quick tips to maintain this level of fitness. Don't bother to take the stairs. Sustain a heavy profile by eating at least three meals and several snacks throughout the day. Sit whenever possible and loaf frequently. Avoid viewing, or worse, engaging with exercise videos. Forsake romantic beach walks. Choose short term over long-term life plans.

Fanatics

Skipping ahead to Fitness Level #3, the *Fanatic*. Don't confuse this level with a professional athlete. Fanatics exercise excessively because they think they will be able to eat whatever they want and still keep excess weight off. Minor decreases in their exercise routine makes them gain weight quickly. Minor surgery or injuries with subsequent activity restrictions often quickly bring forth unwanted pounds.

Another variation of the Fanatics is people who restrict their dietary intake to the extreme (one friend called this the "spit and sawdust diet"). After days of extreme deprivation and discipline, Fanatics like to enjoy a cheat day or two. Sadly, walking two miles before breakfast does not obliterate the excess calories incurred from a bag of chips or a couple of glasses of wine consumed later in the evening while plopped in front of the TV or idly surfing the Net.

Stuffing in food and then purging wasted calories extracts wear and tear on the mind and body. Fanatics give up moderate routines that support a sensible yet enjoyable and healthy lifestyle. Extreme exercise routines, the stuff of an 18 year-old kid's orientation to the military, are a short term "shape up." While it builds physical endurance for combat, it's rarely beneficial as a life long fitness routine.

Jeri has a friend who is an outstanding golfer in her mid 40s. She's a "natural athlete." She looks like the perfect model of fitness but had recently noted the slight beginnings of a "muffin-top" protruding above her slacks. Right after the holidays she went to a gym for the first time in decades.

She started out by pushing her limits to "pump iron" and get back to her high school bench-pressing levels. After two grueling sessions she could barely go to work because of muscle strain and finding that she had gone far beyond her endurance in too short of a time. Rather than quit, she sought the guidance of a physical trainer more in tune with her current situation and goals, and began a more sensible routine.

Know when the risk of a grueling routine outweighs the benefits. Joint damage, stress fractures, muscle tears, and screwed up metabolism are frequent effects of this fitness level. Extreme, uncompromising, militant exercise routines often morph into disordered eating patterns. Some have success, some become ill or injured, and others burnout and simmer back into a *Loafer.*

Optimal Fitness

Level-headed, stable, centered, and happy are ways to describe those who look in the mirror with a wry grin and say, "Not bad, I'm good enough for me and mine." Optimal fitness ("Level 2") still may have persons who yo-yo with their weight, yet many find a place where they can live with their bodies. Optimally fit people are at ease rather than on edge with their bodies. They understand how their bodies function.

Optimal people know what makes them feel better trumps what simply tastes good. Nothing really tastes as good as looking good! They exercise but understand the need for recovery and rest. They have a healthy developed routine based on their bodies and their needs.

The Edge

The line between the high end of level #2 *Optimal Fitness* and the level #3 *Fanatic* is subtle. You can live on the edge if you maintain focus and control. Here's how.

Liz is a client who is consistent and vigilant. She enjoys her family, friends and social activities. She's someone people meet at a party and leave having made a new friend. She's comfortable with her self-assured commitment to fitness. Her weekly routine includes a session with Karen. She spends two additional days doing lifting. Another day is devoted to cardio work that includes walking, jogging, and doing the elliptical. She's on the edge.

So is George. Six days a week he rises early to take a long mindful walk where he finds peace in the morning air. He works out in the gym at least three mornings. He makes time for church every week. He's a salesman who is used to people saying, "I'm not buying." He copes with business travel and work pressure through exercise and a nightly glass of wine—or two. When his belt gets too tight he goes back to a weight loss plan in addition to his daily walks and thrice-weekly workouts. His physician says he has the blood work of a man ten years younger. He's on the edge. He'd still rather his pants didn't keep falling down.

You may need to learn to be comfortable with 10 extra pounds if your body sits at this level of fitness. We're not suggesting that it's better to carry ten extra pounds nor that you should strive to lose only that much, but understand when you're unwilling to stop eating chicken wings you won't improve your fitness level. Increasing your exercise might allow you to eat the wings, but they aren't good for you and the extra 10 reflects unhealthy habits.

We're addressing people who exercise and eat a healthy lean diet but still carry some excess weight. Stop creating more stress just because you have pooches on your belly or under your arms.

Be satisfied when you're doing your best and just keep it up. Disappointment leads people to a destructive workout routine or skipping it altogether. A half a cup is better than a broken one.

"Time lost is not found."

~ Zen

"The funny thing about weight loss is I feel more close to what's left."

~ JAL

Fit Trumps Fat

11

Rather than focus on the foibles of fat, this book addresses being overweight and out of shape through the back door. Fitness. You're not fat—you're just out of shape and detached from your mind-body's needs. Still, the difference between fit and fat is more than just a vowel. We're going to fix fat by becoming fit. Fit trumps fat! Extra weight comes from being out of shape. We need to practice paying attention to the thoughts, feelings, and things we do to let go of extra pounds and hang on to happiness.

Willpower and Radishes

Neuroscience and psychology identified willpower as a hand-me-down. Willpower is a creation of genetics and early childhood training. It's the result of the nurture-nature connections associated with parenting. While overall levels of willpower vary across people, there's a limited quantity of it available at a given moment. We are limited to how much willpower we can expend over a given period of time. It's like a battery that over time needs to be recharged.[25]

Willpower is primarily about effort-full self-control and self-restraint. Willpower involves the focus and energy some of us need to spend on resisting a decadent chocolate bowl of ice cream for dessert. It is an inner drive that pushes you to go to the gym rather than watch a chick flick or slap the snooze button.

Humans are not wired with an abundance of willpower. Unlike long-term memory that has a potentially limitless capacity, we each have only so much willpower to expend at any moment.

Take, for instance, an experiment on willpower that involved three groups of college students charged with completing a puzzle that, unknown to them, was impossible to solve. Two out of three groups were given a special treat to eat right before doing the timed task.

First of all, other research has shown that typical college students detest radishes. You won't find them in many campus salad bars. Students in the first group had to eat a radish before doing the puzzle. The second group was lucky. They had to eat a freshly baked cookie. As for the third group, like the fourth little piggy, they got nothing.

The three groups were timed as they attempted to solve the puzzle. On average, students who had suffered through the radish quit after eight minutes. Students who'd gobbled down the cookies or gone without persisted twice as long as the radish eaters.

So what do radishes and cookies have to do with willpower? Calories? No. Healthy choices? Not at all. Willpower is a resource with limited reserves. The first group tapped the well of "focus and resolve" in order to eat something they perceived as distasteful. They energized will to do something they preferred to avoid. Then

25 J. Gots, *The Neuroscience of Success*. Available online at http://bigthink.com/think-tank/the-neuroscience-of-success

they engaged in a difficult task and found little willpower left to fuel their self-control to push through and solve the problem at hand. They gave up relatively quickly. The two other groups were equally frustrated yet had enough will in stock to persevere twice as long before quitting[26].

Conserve Will

People motivated to lose weight are better off changing their environment to include healthy choices rather than using up their allotment of willpower to resist the urge to scarf down a stack of Oreos. When given the opportunity to eat large quantities of excess food, lab animals stuff themselves. They also get fat. So it is with humans.

There is a way to conserve willpower so that when challenged by raiding the freezer for a pint of Ben and Jerry's Chunky Monkey there is no conflict. Create an environment that frees your mind— don't stock the fridge with slice and bake cookies. Don't fill the grocery cart with junk food. Make a slight alteration to your commutation route to bypass the traffic light in view of your favorite fast food stop.

Brain's hunger sensors are in tune with stomach's fullness as well as with fat and sugar in the bloodstream. If your environment has lots of salad mixings and low-fat soups you'll eat them. You won't really think about it; like the lab animals, you'll eat what's easily accessible. Graze on smaller meals during the day and keep your sugar levels on an even keel.

If you're going to have the will to change your diet and exercise routines, reward your brain for exercising will. Pamper its desire for novel and interesting experiences by finding something besides

---

26 Baumeister, et al. (1998). Ego depletion: Is the active self a limited resource? *Journal of Personality and Social Psychology*, 74(5), 1252–1265,

food to be the center of your life. Placate your brain with new things to think about. Exercise curiosity and you'll discover new ways to enjoy life.

Expect to Change

Before setting a goal for comfortably wearing your ideal size, figure out WHY you want to be that size. Discovering the deep motivation for each goal energizes successful planning. Otherwise you'll become easily distracted. Have you experienced any of these scenarios?

- Got a new plan—heard it from a friend who heard it from a friend that it works really fast.

- Tried it for a whole week. It didn't change the scales. Done.

- Found another friend who had another plan so pitched the first plan for a new plan.

- Frustrated without success—went back to square one and will try to figure this out later.

Doing what you've always done and expecting different results is an oft-quoted definition of insanity. Claim your goals as rightful possessions that frame your fitness plan. Your WHY, the reason you're trying, is the power that ignites each goal. The quest isn't just pursuing the goal of fitness. It is becoming a person who achieves many goals. You will exude confidence through competence. Your persona will reflect self worth. You will trust your gut and your heart to make good choices. It's an identity.

Adjust to Change

Your WHY should be something you dream about. It's more than little daydream. A WHY is your ambition, aspiration, and purpose. Can your goal be to fit into your ideal size? Yes, we suppose it can, but is that the only thing you want to be remembered for in this world? "She was our beloved mother, who wore a size 8."

Discover your goal and create a new level of living. Some people shy away from setting reasonable goals because they fear they aren't worthy or capable of achievement. Too often, in a self-destructive cycle, they set unreasonably difficult goals that exceed their ability and available resources only to fail. Failure is blamed on fate or uncontrollable circumstances. In reality, failure is a successful way to bolster a negative self-image in a self-fulfilling prophecy sort of way. We'd like to adjust and fine-tune our bodies so we can have a better chance of functioning to the best of our abilities and enjoy life.

Karen's job is to work with clients to help them achieve their goals. There were many steps along the way to realizing her career. She didn't see most of them at first. They included getting a job coaching, becoming certified, and expanding her work to other facilities. Along the way she started working on herself. As she taught her clients and listened to her own advice, positive changes took shape. She continues on this path. Karen modifies her plans but doesn't wander or run off course. Sometimes she still steps off the path and deals with distractions and stress factors. Dealing with the death of a pet used to be a darn good reason to grieve with a handful of cookies. Not anymore. She realizes binging will not soothe the nature of grief. It is a refreshed awareness that sustains The ZWL.

It's time to complete your goals worksheet (See Appendix). Make detailed notes about what you want for yourself. Spend time thinking, planning, praying, and asking for guidance. Focus on the driving motivation of your own personal WHY. Learn to counter distractions with a clear focus that you achieve during meditation. Be mindful.

"What is gained is not gained."

~ *Zen Paradox*

*"I'll never lose a thing if
I don't let go of something."*

~ *JAL*

12

You Know So You Do

Think Change

Pick up the pace and proceed on the path to correct thinking.
You know more about you than anyone. Learn how to rely on
yourself as *the* expert on *your* life. Self-understanding involves
becoming intimate with your feelings rather than repressing them.
It also means "getting" how your brain functions and is often
controlled by your feelings rather than your thoughts. Become
open to the reality that body, breath, and mind are inseparable.
Prepare for exercise by taking time to be still in order to manage
personal power that can harness mental activity and energize
your body.

Claim these statements to guide your quest for fitness.

My body is a well-constructed machine. Its purpose is to be a
vehicle for my life on this earth. Food is fuel for the machine
and nourishment for my mind. It is to be savored slowly and
completely. I need less to sustain a healthy energy level, calm
focus, and centered sense of self. The rituals of eating bring forth

good feelings when they are balanced with my body's needs. There are spaces between meals when my mind delights and my body is energized.

I pay attention to how food makes me feel physically and emotionally by keeping a journal while living my personal fitness program. I flourish. I relish the optimal experiences that come from flow of my efforts to become fit.

Avoid reading about other people's diets and begin writing to yourself. Describe what you eat and how eating makes you think about yourself and others. Describe what's on *your* mind. Learn to understand your personal motivation. Set up a ZWL personal routine. Discover that wisdom given graciously though living helps your body thrive.

Brains Want to Know

What do brains want to know? Three things, 1) What things are, 2) How things can be used, and 3) why it's important to know both. The ZWL challenges your brain to know how it works. We cover this by providing exercise routines and explaining fitness levels. As we discussed about mindfulness, learning becomes rich and non-conscious as we use whole and parts at the same time. Brains crave feedback that evaluates whether its efforts to meet challenges were successful.

Brains have the lifelong ability to reorganize their neural pathways based on new experiences. As we learn about fitness and acquire new information about exercise, mindfulness, and nutrition our brains are rewired. As we become wiser protectors of our mind-body, persistent functional changes happen in our brains. These physical, chemical, and electrical changes represent our new knowledge. We become a new improved version of our former selves. Our reorganized brains are constructed to stick with exercise and healthy habits that keep our bodies and brains fit.

Tend to your new mind-body as you would a child. Be caring of its preferences and provide amply opportunities to regularly exercise these preferences. The brain is a ruthless pruner—it eliminates pathways that are not frequently traveled. We forget what we do not hold to our heart. It's critical to hold to the hallmarks of your ZWL plan and keep the flow between fitness and heath well traveled in the brain.

> *"Moderation. Small helpings. Sample a bit of everything. These are the secrets of happiness and good health."*
>
> *~ Julia Child*

> *"Less is more, more or less."*
>
> *~ JAL*

13

From Nuked to Slow Food

Growing Slowly

There is a growing trend in Italy called Slow Food. The movement is the somewhat anti-fast food. Italians eat and drink their meals very unhurriedly. Diners proceed through a meal slowly savoring its aroma, visual appeal, taste and the company in which it is shared. Leisurely meals are enjoyed as stress-down experiences. Conversation is abundant. The combination of food and companionship satisfies one's physical and emotional hungers.

Visualize

A sense of calm and peacefulness are functions of happiness. Let's do a short visualization exercise and focus on the simple pleasure inherent in a good meal. Imagine sitting around a dining table with good friends and family. Cell phones and TVs are turned off. The table is set in an appealing way. Immediately your brain is processing memories of pleasant dining experiences, real and imagined. Inhale the delightful aromas in anticipation of the first bite. Relax. There is no rush here. Grasp pleasure in the moment. Eat smaller bites. Chew longer. Enjoy the meal as long as you like.

Are you feeling a touch uncomfortable because of worries about eating too much and populating those fat colonies? Don't be. By eating slowly we consume less food. Let's go back to Einstein again. Time is relative. By taking more time to eat, the body's digestive process extends beyond the time it takes (about 20 minutes) for the brain to de-activate the hunger drive. The gazelles of the dining set eat so fast they clean their plate while the hunger switch is still in the on position. The brain drives them right into second helpings.

Slothfulness

Slower eaters realize when their appetite has been satiated and stop eating whether or not their plate is empty. During Jeri's last visit to Italy there were no overweight diners to be seen at any of the restaurants. Granted, most Italians do a great deal of walking, much more than just the few paces from a parking space to the front door. A meal was a dining experience whether it was simple fare or a gourmet plate. Each was an exquisite balance of protein, fresh fruits and vegetables. Dining hours slipped easily through evening and settled the deep cushion of late night.

There is little enjoyment gained by rushing through a meal. Consider instead that changing one's eating habits from grabbing a bite to savoring a meal as mindful exercise. If you can't let go of a Type A driven personality that must always be doing something goal oriented, consider the extra chewing and talking as burning calories. Either work at letting loose or give yourself permission to relax. Avoid grab and go eating opportunities whenever possible. Twenty minutes per meal is all your brain is asking.

We've become a microwave society. Technological advances have done little to slow the hectic pace of life. In an effort to make things easier we've just complicated life. We expect instant gratification and are unwilling or unable to wait for results. Children have issues with learning for the same reasons. Have you seen the merchandise imprinted "Sail Fast, Live Slow"? That's exactly what we're encouraging you to do. The success of a ZWL program depends establishing a pace you can sustain.

Garden Secrets

If you're not inclined to be a gardener at least consider amping up your culinary skills. Watch the Food Network to learn simple cooking skills. Download recipes from episodes that tickle your taste buds. Consider taking a free cooking class at Williams Sonoma[27]. You can learn how to combine flavors, textures, and presentations to create dining experiences. Educate your palate and surprise your brain with new taste sensations.

Jeri has two rules about family dining. No fast food for dinner, and sit down together to enjoy dinner. Dinnertime is a family ritual and a celebration of the small things in life. The table is set with colorful place mats or cloth. Candlelight dinners aren't reserved for romantic occasions. Candles are lit every night. She often takes photos of food as it's being chopped, blended, grilled, and sautéed. She caps the photo stream with a shot of the complete meal when it is served.[28]

---

27 Visit Williams Sonoma on line to find a class near you, http://www.williams-sonoma.com/customer-service/store-events.html

28 Jeri has a blog that includes a photo documentary of her Julia and Jeri Sunday Supper at http://web.me.com/jerilevesque/Site/Julia_%26_Jeri.html

Feed Your Head

We are what we eat and our brains are really hogs at the trough. While human brains only weigh about three pounds (pick up a bag of sugar) they scoop up 25% of the calories consumed during any given day. Food is to our emotions as drugs are to a junkie; it makes us feel better or worse, sleepy or stoked, fulfilled or wasted. Our diets influence all aspects of our lives from health to appearance. Mind-bodies need plenty of water, good fats and carbs, a bounty of fresh vegetables and fruit, a modicum of sugar, and a lot less than we'd like to think of sugar, caffeine, and alcohol.

Pace Yourself

Teaching preschoolers taught Karen a lot about taking life at a slower pace. Kids march to an inner beat with unique rhymes and rhythms yet their short legs cover lots of territory. We've found three steps for approaching a healthy lifestyle:

1. Pause—observe, be, proceed

2. Breathe—three deep breaths and listen

3. Be grateful—say thank you for whatever you face

We like the idea of less involved meditations during the day. Jon Kabat-Zinn describes meditation as "falling awake" that creates new brain structures.[29] Give your morning routine a quiet boost. Greet the morning with a stretch in bed before your feet hit the floor. Listen to your partner breathing or the birds awakening. Take three deep breaths and give thanks. Easy, right? This is something you'll develop as a habit. Get in your car and before you turn the key in the ignition—STOP. Take three deep breaths and listen—the

---

29 See the YouTube Video, "Mindfulness with Jon Kabat-Zim" for a meditation workshop presented to Google employees. Http://www.youtube.com/watch?v=3nwwKbM_vJc

keys swing and click, the garage door squeaks while it opens, and the day begins. Now give thanks. Then start the car and drive towards your day.

When Karen's oldest son was three, she asked him to pick up his room while she straightened the house. Ten minutes later he was sitting in the middle of his room putting puzzles together. Karen watched for a minute while resisting the impulse to run in there and clean. Karen asked why he was putting the puzzle together? He kept working and said, "Well, I have to put the puzzle together before I can put it on the shelf."

Karen wanted the job done. Her son wanted to do the job his own way. She only wanted to see results while he was engrossed in the process of doing his work rather than being done. Jeri sees this as a lot like sailing. The voyage is often more fun than arriving at the dock. Life is a process for which weight loss is not the end result.

A fast pace and instant gratification can also cause disappointment. A body is not going to change overnight. Changes happen over time. There will be an adjustment period relative to how long your system's been neglected or abused before lasting results are realized. The change you seek is intended to last for a long time. Start the chain of change by relaxing and being conscious.

Be Still

Now, where are you? Can you tune in to your environment? Understanding the space you occupy can lead to greater self-understanding. Consciousness or mind-fullness is what you need to achieve balance within and around. It's what moves us away from the instant answers and nudges us to the patient, waiting part of life.

Go through a day being conscious of your senses, actions and feelings. Take a deep breath before you eat, drink or pick up the phone. You don't need to make any judgments about what you see, hear or feel. Recognize the present for what it is. This will help you in setting up your program. Trust yourself.

Meditation isn't for everyone. Listening and observing is for all. If you have never found it conducive to sit with your eyes closed and wait on nirvana you are not alone. Don't write off meditation as something you cannot do. It is possible for everyone in a thousand different ways. Here are a few:

sitting on the beach

walking alone

fishing

star gazing

sitting empty

thinking nothing

being still

staring through a window

seeing behind your eyes

watching the ocean

Meditation is a form of non-doing. It involves not wanting anything else at the moment. People meditate when they are running, cooking, and even making love. It's a sense of being completely focused on a moment of being. The key to meditative non-thinking is to be comfortable with your self. Be alone and just watch. Draw no conclusions about what you see. Try to post no thoughts. Just watch the world around you. Be patient and allow your mind to take a holiday. Daily meditation will help you to control eating habits and stay on track with your fitness program.

We might not have time everyday to meditate. Fine tune time and you'll learn to better enjoy life. Take pleasure in the lightness of your being as your weight comes down and you sense becoming more centered. Rather than nuke your life, learn to "Live Slow."

"Those who know others are wise.
Those who know themselves are enlightened."

~ The Tao Te Ching

"Dinner time."

~ JAL

Loss

"We shape clay into a pot,
   but it is the emptiness inside
   that holds whatever we want."

~ Lao Tsu

14

Eat Zen Like

Some of us haven't thought about how to eat food since we were little kids. And, our grandmas might shake a finger at us for forgetting our manners! Sadly, it's become quite common for children to enter kindergarten having never eaten a meal at a table or used common utensils. These kids are products of the fast food culture where meals come wrapped in paper and eaten with our bare hands.

Minding Manners

Some parents don't teach their children to chew with their mouths closed. Meals are rushed to accommodate TV schedules, sports practice, homework, and appointments. Basic manners dictate the importance of eating slowly, closing one's mouth when chewing, not talking with a mouth full of food, and putting the fork down between bites. These are not the morés of our fast food culture. They are grandma's rules for slow food that was lovingly prepared and shared as a binding element that defined the family as a social unit.

Just as food that is balanced with texture, color and flavors appeals to our aesthetic senses, our fellow diners should also trigger our sense of pleasure rather than repulsion. When eating, let's slow down a bit to remember the essential attributes of proper dining.

Always sit when you eat anything, even a snack. Even jackals refrain from running when devouring a carcass. Put down your fork between bites. It does nothing to provide balance so you don't fall of your chair. A fork is not a mini-version of Neptune's Trident. It isn't designed to fend off rude attempts by others to steal the food off your plate. It's not only polite; it gives your body time to digest.

Food digestion begins with the first bite and flows through chewing. Chewing titillates the taste buds. The taste buds send signals to the brain that life is either good or its time to hurl. Besides initiating the pleasure principals so dear to eating, the alchemy of turning a broccoli spear into energy and an éclair into fat takes a few moments.

Chewing allows insulin to be released into the food to aid digestion rather than roll off the wad you hurriedly stuffed into your gut. If the insulin doesn't mix into the food as it goes into the digestive system you'll continue to feel hungry as your blood sugar continues to drop. Slow down! Don't use the fork as a pitchfork to slam more fat into the liver's warehouse of lost lipids.

Hydrate

Drink plenty of water throughout the day. The brain's mechanism that indicates thirst is very closely related to the center that triggers hunger. It's easy to confuse the "Hey I'm dry as a bone" signal with the hunger drive. Properly hydrated people know when they are hungry. It's a learned behavior for many of us.

The rule of thumb that can teach the water vs. food choice is the color of your urine. It should be almost clear. If you can read a newspaper through it then you know you are getting enough. Visualize this rather than pee in a glass and try to read the Op Ed section of USA Today. Try to stay clear of plastic water bottles and use instead a stainless steel or aluminum bottle. Yes, that was a Zen like minder of being green like Kermit.

> **NOTE:** Some people can do well to eat less and this is where we start the process of listening to our bodies. Be certain you are truly hungry before you eat. Don't push this to the extreme when your hands start to shake and you feel woozy. You'll only panic and thrust food down your throat. First drink water. Pause a moment as the water fuels your thinking cells. Still feeling hungry? Eat. Slowly savor the pleasure of eating.

Timed to Eat

Set a timer if you often forget to eat. This will help you to consume some food at regular intervals and keep your blood sugar on an even keel. Snacks should be small and meals moderate in size. Don't act like there will be no tomorrow. It takes very little to fuel your body. Choose healthy, visually appealing and tasty yet healthy snacks that are lean on fat and sugar. As they are, you shall be.

If at all possible don't eat after dinner. The accepted formula is to have nothing after 7 p.m. That isn't always possible because of activities and commuting. If you eat late, try to wait a least an hour before you fall into bed.

Share the human experience of dining with those you can tolerate and those whose company you enjoy. You might even find that you eat better, eat somewhat less, and enjoy eating more when you are with other people. Big surprise!

"Meaning and reality were not hidden somewhere behind things, they were in them, in all of them."

~ Siddhartha, by Hermann Hesse

"If I cook, I am going to enjoy wine with dinner. If you cook, I'll bring the wine. Either way it's fine."

~ JAL

The Power of Food

15

Is your relationship with food one of your most closely guarded secrets? Do you ever share with a friend a confidential revealing of how food makes you feel? Do you find it somewhat mysterious that you can't think of a single word that best represents the greatest barrier between you and delicious yet healthy choices?

Connect or Disconnect?

For some folks, how they eat, how often they eat, and what they eat is a rather clandestine part of their lives. People seem to clamor rather boisterously just after the holidays about their new gym memberships and those great new diets. The issue becomes somewhat hush-hush as the weeks roll by and winter yields to spring. The secret about food is to know whether it has power over you or visa versa. But how are these secrets revealed? At what point does one know who's the boss?

When we press a pencil to paper or click open a new word-processor document, we can confront what we know about how, when, and why we do that basic function simply known as eating.

Going Past Barriers

Start doodling and writing about barriers between you and weight loss in your food journal. What do the barriers look like? Can you imagine a brick wall that prevents you from reaching your goals? Perhaps it's time to doodle a way to get around, over, or under that wall. Chip away at the mortar that holds the bricks together? Blow it up? Hmm—it's your barrier—let your imagination soar. Once you've destroyed the barrier, doodle a fresh healthy image. Scribble your way to that healthy vision of your new and fit body.

Craving

We've talked about how our brains are wired to avoid threats and are attracted to pleasures. Neuroscientists explain behavior in terms of chemical responses and electrical activity. They explain why people crave food such as hot fudge sundaes by pointing out dopamine's powerful role in pleasurable feelings. People just talk about how good it tastes.

While our brains are wired for enjoyment there are also many pathways for wanting. Liking and wanting are companions. We like the things we want. When these two feelings are balanced we're okay. It's when the brain starts building too many circuits for wanting that the wiring for liking wears thin. We want more and oddly enough, like what we get less and less. The brain boost the charges in the wanting circuits hoping to grab the pleasure it craves. Then, just as for many people, the chase is better than the catch—there's a let down.

There's an old marketing slogan for potato chips that followed this line of brain activity, "I'll bet you can't eat just one." The psychology in play was addiction. Eating just a single chip triggered a craving for more. The appetite wasn't quelled by a handful; the packages grew in size to accommodate the lust for more. The same cocktail of dopamine, brain wiring, and bad habits grounds an alcoholic's understanding that, "one is too many and ten's not enough."

Journal daily. List all the food you eat. Note your feelings while going about the business of eating. Play with words. Think of all the words you know to describe feelings.

Here are a few:

elated	depleted
stupendous	loved
happy	satiated
frustrated	guilty
free	courageous

What action words describe the way you eat?

grazing	munching
hovering	slurping
gnawing	nibbling

Or do you

chomp	snarf
smack	blitz
sip	grind

What animal reminds you of the mental image of yourself during mealtime?

gazelle	lion
dolphin	hyena
finch	raccoon

What does eating sound like?

bells ringing	backhoe digging
volcano erupting	snow falling
mill wheel grinding	river raging
mother's lullaby	

What motivated the consumption of the last food to pass your lips?

hunger	boredom
anxiety	an urge
an aroma	a dinner bell
the appointed time on the clock	

At some point write down the reactions you had to the food you ate. Did you get sleepy? Feel stuffed? Still unsatisfied?

Were you thinking about what tastes delighted your palate? Timing how long it was till your next fix (meal)? Were you hungry sooner or could you last until the next meal?

Want Not, Forget Not

We tend to forget about quick snacks gulped down on the way to meetings. Sometimes we're ambushed by donuts and sweets set nicely out beside the office coffee. Seemingly defenseless, we grab one and scarf it down with a slug of latte. Funny though how many dieters talk about "let's just stop for a quick bite." That's a bit like a vampire saying, "Just a quick sip." Eating on the fly, disguising a snack loaded with sugar and fat as a "bite" are futile attempts to diminish the power of food over our bodies and minds. Visualize eating on a fly, and you may well forsake the urge to eat on the fly.

The detrimental effects of snack attacks leave us unguarded and suppliant. This is especially true when eating food that's a cheap grade of fuel for the body's engine. Engine knocking becomes tightness in the chest felt when climbing stairs. Another after effect is the creepy sensation that movie theater seats aren't as wide as they used to be. You start to hear the whisper of words like "lumber" rather than "dash" to describe the first trip from the bed to the bathroom every morning. Karen, a recovering bulimic, has shared her delusional thinking about eating. Is a donut out of sight really out of mind, or is it a blur on its way to the fat cells' waistline holding tank? Or, did it act as a stealth bomber, undetected by the brain's warning system to avoid all things harmful to the mind-body?

A trainer called Karen to consult on a client who never lost weight. The trainer brought 20 sheets of workouts she had written over the last 4 months. Despite a rigorous exercise regimen the client hadn't dropped pounds or inches. Karen felt the workouts were appropriate. She asked what the client said about her diet. The trainer replied, "She *says* she eats like a bird." Well, we know that a bird eats at least half their weight in food each day! Obviously the client wasn't being honest with her trainer or herself. This bird was eating too much to fly and was miserable. Her spirits were grounded and she blamed the trainer.

The client agreed to keep an honest, accurate food log for the next month. She tracked amount, type, and frequency of foods she consumed daily in her journal. She painted a clear image of an unbalanced lifestyle. She could not expend enough to burn excess food. She wasn't balancing her fitness program.

Writing opened the client's awareness of what really went into her mouth; "I just ate chicken" was not fully accurate. She didn't mean a grilled boneless, skinless chicken breast. She was eating an order of buffalo chicken wings! Yes, she ate the side of celery too. In earlier self-reports she didn't mention her habit of dipping each stalk in a thick glob of blue cheese to tame the spicy wings' heat. Writing helped the clients, and will you to understand yourself and be understood by others.

Track your eating in writing. It will make you accountable. One of Karen's clients found she was always writing about what she bypassed at the salad bar, "I skipped the croutons and the desserts!" What she didn't write was, "Big scoop of creamy cottage cheese, Chinese dried noodles and a few salted pumpkin seeds, just a touch of the cheddar cheese and not very much blue cheese dressing."

Power Struggles

A candid written account of your dietary habits puts the buck exactly where it should be—in your head. An eating log represents your choices, whether they were mindful or impulsive; you had the power to choose. It's your life. Feel empowered regarding food. Remember the old 1960's mantra, "We are what we eat."

Stop swooning over chocolate desserts and thick steaks. You can only cuddle with a slice of chocolate cake for so long, and a day-old piece leftover steak looks, well, old and nasty. Nothing that is consumed and turned to waste within a day should have power over one's mind and body. Becoming emotionally attached to something is to grant it power over yourself.

Why should you care about power? Let's take a moment to play with semantics: here's what's called a cognitive map of how many brains "think" about the word power.

Who's in charge? You or the drive-thru menu options? Your mind or the 16-year-old kid who serves up supersized caramel lattes at the gas station? Your body that has managed to stretch and flex to accommodate your dietary habits or the agribusiness complex that pumps extra chemical and fats into foods to make them last longer and taste better?

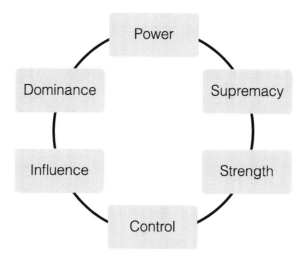

Think about the power of preservatives. A Twinkie with an indeterminate shelf life isn't going away any time soon just because it found its way past your lips.

If you think you aren't a superhero, you're wrong. Each person is a power to be reckoned with. Allowing one's focus to be swayed by food and taste and brief, fleeting senses of satisfaction is to give that power away. Imagine granting authority to a truffle, or acknowledging the dominance of a triple beef burger with bacon and cheese.

As George Lucas, through the Star Wars character Qui Gon advised young Anakin, *"Always remember, your focus determines your reality."* The point of this chapter is that if you want to become fit and trim you must give power to a clear focus on being fit and trim. Focus in order to make weight loss and fitness the reality of your life. Make decisions relative to eating, dining, and consuming nutrition to sustain your mind and body. Choose to keep your focus on being fit, trim, and healthy.

Center

Keep a focus on ZWL by writing about your personal power to become trim and fit. Read your own words that echo your desires to reach a personal best. It's not easy. It takes time and discipline. You have to persevere in order for your body and mind to carry on what best supports a clear focus on fitness and mental well-being. Let your journal flow around you. Use sticky notes with cryptic messages to yourself on the bathroom mirror, dashboard, and inside the kitchen cabinet. Focus on positive messages! When you don't seem to remember what they said, write a new message to yourself. Post visual images of your fitness goal, such as Nicole Kidman on the Red Carpet or Pierce Brosnan sipping a "shaken not stirred" martini.

Visualize images of your fitness goal. A redwood tree, granite cliff, or that magnificent waterfall off that big mountain in Africa. Focus on the now, right now.

Think hard and clearly enough and soon enough, with much energy focused on a precise goal. The reflection in the mirror will be what you want to see. The secret of food is that if you control it, you can command it to serve you for all of your days. Hail to the Chief!

"Be with just this."

~ Zen

"Love what you eat so that you may eat what you love."

~ JAL

16

Eat Love Prey

Hunting involves tracking wildlife for food. Gardening involves planting, tending, and harvesting flora for food. Either way, what is sought is gone once found. Experienced hunters make sure not to become disoriented and lost in the woods. That's when "turn about is fair play" and the hunter becomes prey. At a very basic level, whether vegetarian or omnivore, people need to keep track of what they eat. This involves more than giving a squint and sniff test to the furry contents of refrigerated leftovers. Tracking involves orienting ourselves to the choices we make about what we eat.

Keep Moving

Commercially sponsored diets frequently recommend minimizing caloric intake or avoiding certain foods completely. Nature demands balance and so does your body. The great question of equilibrium is, how much of what food group is enough to satiate a healthy appetite, sustain high energy levels and personal comfort, yet not contribute to ill health effects? The answer is, Fulfillment depends on how much you move.

Einstein had it right when he mused that, "Life is like riding a bicycle. To keep your balance you must keep moving." Kids don't learn to ride a bike by watching a YouTube video; they get on a bike and move! Movement also involves forward thinking.

Hunters establish a home base or rendezvous point before tracking. Ever been lost in a Wal-Mart supercenter when tracking down a particular product? The easiest way to orient oneself is to figure the check out counters. Maybe this is a "senior moment" caused by not paying attention.

Tracking one's dietary habits requires motivation, effort, and focus. Readers might shrug off this book because, "weight loss, food, and exercise doesn't apply to me" because, "I'm a little out of shape".

A friend of ours is a Nurse Practitioner. She says that one of the first things overweight and obese patients ask is, "Do you think I have a thyroid problem?" This isn't a chapter on self-diagnosis. If you think you have a physical problem associated with uncontrollable dietary habits write a note in your food journal to make a doctor's appointment to ask about any condition you *think* you might have.

Pay attention to your head's view of your body's status. It might be on target or, it might be dodging the obvious. Schedule a wellness and prevention check up or an out-of-pocket expense to a nearby community clinic. Also understand that Internet doctors are not able to diagnose individual issues as accurately because they can't see you and peel past the layers of excuses and denial you might have regarding a health history.

Tracking

The ZWL is designed to teach you to call the shots about what your body needs. We're supporting your quest to establish at a livable arrangement between yourself and the world though a reasonable balance of diet and exercise. Again, the task is to track your food intake and note how different food makes you feel. Pay attention to how you focus on the hunt finding Internet bargains, choosing the right food for the occasion—rather special or just a midweek repast.

Try to describe the capture:

- At the store, reusable or plastic bags?

- Once home store it in the pantry or fridge? or

- Eaten whole, immediately, when caught!

Dress Up

Next, as a tracker who successfully bagged its prey, or a gardener upon harvest, focus on dressing your catch. How do you consume? Do any of these descriptions fit?

- Careful not to drip on the suit when driving the car.

- Sure not to spill during a business meeting.

- Carefully handled near the laptop.

- Juggled when tending to toddlers?

- Can't remember crashing on the couch.

There's another side to dressing food as well. Do you alphabetize your spices so they are readily available to add certain tastes to meats, poultry, seafood, and vegetables? Do you marinate, braise, blanch, brine, or otherwise add spices and herbs to fresh meats and vegetables? Are there certain rituals you observe about kneading, baking, braising, stewing, roasting, and grilling? Track and analyze the hunt, capture, and dressing of food for two weeks.

Challenge

Here's a dietary challenge after living the ZWL for about three weeks. Try to eliminate foods that are most often reported as antagonistic by people who have issues with their digestion and metabolism. Removing all these foods at once and then and introducing them one at a time is the oldest tool physicians use for figuring out the effects of each.

The goal is to better understand which foods don't work with your body and which make your toes glow. As you re-introduce foods into your diet, make an assessment of how your body reacts. If you think you might have an underlying condition such as food allergies, check in with your physician. Ask for a "stamp of encouragement" for you to work out and eat healthy with no fad diets with any restrictions. Strive to achieve moderation, wellness, fitness, mood elevation, appetite satisfaction, and great odds for a long and happy life.

When your notebook looks rich and full of "food for thought", begin a food analysis. Try restricting the following the "testy" foods from your diet.

- Stay clear of refined sugar.
- If you use honey, use raw honey.
- Sweeten with Stevia.

> **"Testy" food.** Food that remains in the body long past digestion in the form of uninvited fat! Like a houseguest that won't leave!

Tracking the Effects of Food

Let me explain how sugar affects me. I get nuts. I begin to find little things in my husband that bother me. My children get on my last nerve. I wonder, why I am even bothering to keep working at my job? I don't want to hurt others or myself, I just want to run away and play on a beach somewhere. Watch your reactions and be slow when you introduce sugar into your diet again.

~ Karen

Cut back on **Gluten (breads and pastas).** Gluten is found in wheat, rye and barley. It's often processed into other products. Gluten free diets are the rage right now, but as your Mom would warn, "If everyone is jumping off a cliff, do you have to fall head first into the rocks below too?"

Shy away from **Dairy products**. Why? They are higher in calories. Big surprise! Two reasons for eliminating dairy is to help you see immediate results by eating foods that are lower in calories. Do you get a quick buzz on feeling lighter in your flip-flops? Statistically, more people have digestive issues with dairy products than with many other food groups. Check your food journal and gauge your body's responses during and after eating dairy. If the results are dramatic, sudden bloating, cramping, and unpredictable colon blows, consider eliminating dairy from most of your diet. You are the best judge of what your body tolerates and celebrates.

The ZWL Tracking Food Plan is two weeks of unrestricted eating with daily entries into the food journal, followed by two weeks of restricting sugar, gluten, and dairy. Reintroduce each food item one per week and track your mind and body's responses. Leaving behind gluten and dairy forever is not being suggested here. Cutting out something forever isn't necessarily best for you. Decide which foods are testy foods and cut them out of your diet. You may need to eliminate other foods than these few we are restricting here. Pay attention to how you feel.

After Taste

By tracking your food, it is possible to find out just what you eat that you lust for and that which you loathe. In the course of a typical day you may well eat out of habit. You might fear of losing the right to choose something "forbidden." Sometimes "bad" food is there at a moment when options are not apparent. Tracking food may enlighten you about the balance between you and food that in turn may release your fears about the effects of eating what pleases or terrifies you most.

The ZWL is not about starving one's gut in the name of a size 0 little black dress or teeny red Speedo. The discipline of these self-study journaling exercises is nourishment that enhances efforts to become fit, trim, and healthy. The object of the proverbial hunt is to track and consume food that nourishes and nurtures your body mind and spirit.

Sliver to Slice

Food that a body cannot process well tends to make the eater feel depressed and tired. It's no wonder one of the great product ads of the '50s was "Mmmmmm good"—food diets (or food choices) impact motivation, mood, memory, and mental processing. Food choices can enhance or deflate mental concentration. Diet can also be the *Timothy Leary Experience* ('He'll take you up—he'll bring you down.")[30] which makes you feel like a disoriented passenger

---

on his astral plane. If you consume food as a proper fuel you can enhance your brain's capacity to think and feel good.

Of course some food plays to our desires for immediate gratification, such as a journal entry that might state:

It looked so good I just had to have it—and one bite wasn't enough to satisfy my longing—so I had some more. And then, it was gone. Sadly, I didn't feel any more satisfied than if I'd just pushed myself away from the dessert tray.

Slab to Slob

Look at the emotions drawn into the choice of eating a slab of chocolate cake! Desire, longing, loss, sadness, guilt, frustration, and anger are common emotions associated with controlling one's diet. What we are discussing is emotional intelligence as it applies to food. The term emotional intelligence (EI) refers to what Daniel Goldstein identified as "an ability to validly reason with emotions and to use emotions to enhance thought."[31] We're viewing EI as a way to think about food in constructive ways that enhance your emotional wellbeing and fitness.

If you have no control when chocolate is sitting on the table, make a rational decision to stay away from chocolate for a while. Set a reasonable goal and focus on the satisfaction of being in control—choose other foods that satisfy your craving for sweets. Research shows that a little bit of sugar sharpens decision-making— how much is little is another quirk on relativity. Carbs can soothe our minds—it's no accident that comfort foods represent lots of different pastas (mac 'n cheese) and breads (fresh baked or toasted). The chemicals they represent fire up the limbic (emotional) centers of our brains.

---

31 Daniel Goleman, *Emotional Intelligence: Why it Can Matter More than IQ.* (1995). NY, NY:Bantam.

Go Figure

Make note of the foods you need to avoid. From a rational standpoint your body can't burn them off. Besides, they aren't as appealing stored in a derriere. We're not steering you toward a monastic life of sacrifice—figure out what foods make you feel great from the first tinge of anticipation to the final results of how your body looks and feels over time. Explore for new foods—start in the fresh fruits and vegetables aisle. Initiate your palate to new sensations. Don't let this phase of the process get past you. It's a vital step in your fitness path toward health.

We're realists and understand human nature. As TV's Dr. Greg House says, "Everybody lies." When it comes to changing dietary habits folks tend to "give a little" when it comes to honest reckoning about what they consume. Expect to experiment and eat foods you know aren't good for you. Keep track of your body and minds' responses to new foods and different combinations of old favorites. Record the way you feel physically (stuffed, crampy, light, energized) and emotionally (satisfied, crummy) as clear signals about how well your body is in or out of balance.

Disequilibrium is that nasty sense of imbalance where thoughts, emotions, and body fitness are struggling with disharmony. A body not operating in balance is open for illness and disease. Restoring balance is something to think about, act upon, and reflect on all in the name of fitness and wellbeing over the course of a long life.

Work with your Emotional Intelligence. Don't punish yourself either. Let it go. Hold no grudges or animosity toward yourself when personal reflection reveals disequilibrium. People with high levels of emotional intelligence tend to have more satisfying social relationships. They understand how emotions make people click. When applied to diet, emotional intelligence can be used to build more positive relationships between you and food.

Pick up your ZWL journal and write about food, *again*. Explain to yourself why you ate a second helping of smashed potatoes in the first place. What happened during the day that might have ticked you off? Weigh the pleasure of an edible moment against the hours spent exercising. Then decide if it was really worth it. It doesn't mean you've had your last Girl Scout Thin Mint—we're suggesting that eating an entire sleeve of them before bed is not a wise and balanced choice.

This is where you should be in the ZWL program:

- Regular daily movement = exercise.

- Following a fitness routine three to five days a week, depending on your beginning fitness level.

- Keeping a ZWL food journal to identify the foods your mind-body churns into high energy, jubilant spirits, and a sense of fitness.

We can't itemize the number of things that will make you eat the wrong foods. Common sense and moderation are probably the two keys to a balance that harmonizes your emotions, mental sharpness, and physical fitness. There are things that'll throw you in a tizzy. A box of your favorite candy magically appears at Valentine's Day—it's gone before President's Weekend, and you're at the gym 12 times before St. Patrick's Day. That's not so bad is it? You spend a workout for each piece of chocolate? And the feel good sensations of a good burn during a cardio work out? Balance. That's the ticket.

Triggers

Everybody has a set of impulsive triggers. Your emotional intelligence helps you filter whether these triggers are helpful or harmful. Some people discern the difference with great sophistication while others simply are clueless. Impulsive triggers energize choices to gobble up high fat, salty, and carb-laden snacks when you aren't even hungry. We all know the triggers to our own guns. We also know what ammo we have to stave off bad choices. If you haven't thought of it before, give yourself a minute and think about them now. Do you sense an immediate desire to fight or take flight? These are negative triggers—they take aim at your mental, emotional, and physical health.

Reflect on these and other questions in your ZWL journal. What makes you feel the need to eat? Wait too long between meals? Plummeting sugar levels send powerful distress signals to the brain that instill a minor emotional meltdown that stimulates over eating. Stress, anger, resentment, and sometimes joy are emotions that can elicit a food response.

Look at your journal and think about the last meal you ate, or the last snack, or the food you are chewing right now. What made you feel you had to have that food? If it was genuinely hunger, explain to yourself how you knew you were really hungry. What signals did your body send to your brain that drove you to try and satiate the hunger drive?

Sometimes we can't get back to a place the same way we came. You have to try different routes—some easier and others more convoluted. If you occasionally skip the gym, forego the 20-minute walk and gorge on a bean burrito, the path is going to become steeper. You're could become frustrated if you start believing that the ZWL is getting harder rather than more routine. If you keep to the path without feeling resentment, the journey will be more pleasant. Psychotherapists help their patients understand that given a choice between two paths—one easy the other difficult—if a vision of the journey's end is upheld either choice is okay. You'll get to where you want to be. How you get there is not as important as the final arrival at your destination.

We hope you choose the healthier path, but recognize how a myriad of feelings can derail your attempts to heal yourself. Emotionally charged circumstances sometimes lead to a cul-de-sac in your journey, and non-productive feelings. Eating can be your attempt to fill the hollow space within. Compulsive eating won't fill that void. Cravings are relentless. Yet, you can hear in your head the voice of your mother or spouse telling you pigging out isn't a good idea. These warnings fail to prevent a downward spiral of negative thinking that culminates with self-condemnation—a feeling of greater emptiness that can only be lulled with more food. With addiction, the buffers in the brain between impulse and action are thwarted. Recovery is a complex process of rewiring neural pathways.

If this chapter speaks to you, affirm your will to achieve your personal fitness goals. Admit that arm wrestling a buffalo chicken wing always beats your resolve. Defeat leads to a side of waffle fries and extra cheese on the burger. Some among us are addicted to food. This is an unhealthy obsession or dependence on eating that yields personal control to organic matter. This compulsion can dominate thinking and release impulses to satiate the desire to bite, chew and swallow food. Any form of addiction severely alters brain areas critical to decision-making, learning and memory, and behavior control.

Food addiction manifests itself as not just an abnormal craving for copious amounts of food but also a craving for foods that are harmful. When you constantly eat even when you're not hungry and feel guilty after overeating, or lie about everything related to your diet—chances are you have developed a psychological dependence on food. These dependencies vary but signal a loss of control.

There is no easy way to deal with a food addiction. It is an illness that knows no gender, age, or economic boundaries. It is a psychological and physical illness that, left untreated, brings forth more severe effects including depression and obesity. The first step is to admit the problem exists and the next is to seek medical intervention and psychological support. For many, these steps are best taken knowing that you walk the path with a higher power.

Keep in mind our discussion about approaching and avoiding certain things that aren't really good for us. Even when the initial experience is horrifying, such as "I ate so much I threw up all over myself," residual memories of the craving and satisfaction will seduce one's will when ever the two shall meet. Contained within each bite is the memory of all the times you ate this when you were not well. Accept this situation as an imperative to make an appointment with your physician to discuss and treat your addiction.

There is no shame in wanting to conquer an illness or to stake a claim as a recovered food addict. Focus on what you have to gain by acknowledging your loss of control. You will begin to fill that empty space you once thought of as hunger with a new, healthy sense of "you."

Emotional Intelligence in Action

You might benefit from writing about your emotional state along side each food choice in your journal. Reflecting on the emotional responses to food choices helps us connect with ingrained habits and alerts us to our emotional relationship with different foods. Enhancing your emotional intelligence about eating is a very important step toward health.

If you write "tired" next to each dinner entry, you probably work hard, endure a hectic commute, and always feel tired by supper. Fire up that engine! Pack a snack for mid-afternoon fuel shortages. Know what satisfies your "got to eat or die" urgency without sacrificing a slow food experience an hour our so later—when you can relax and savor your meal. We're not talking about grabbing a quick PB&J or even half a sandwich—an extra lunch is not a snack. A snack might consist of 2 peanut butter crackers, a ¼ cup of cottage cheese, cheese stick, ¼ cup of raw almonds, or a piece of fruit. That added food mid-afternoon would keep your hunger under control. It's an emotionally satisfying relationship between you and your meal plans.

Many people eat when they are upset or disappointed. If you find any other emotion attached to your hunger, DO NOT EAT until after you journal about that feeling. First wash away the bad feelings with a glass of water. Water will help you think ahead of your powerful emotional processing. Write out why you are so angry or upset and tell it all! If you are upset about something at work, blast away. You can't hurt anyone and it will help you feel better. You might even discover your hunger is gone after you deal with your emotion.

Emotional intelligence is something that can be built over time. It's not a trait we are locked into at any particular level. However, poor eating and exercise habits leave us feeling down and dumb. Emotional intelligence is critical for helping us process information—and when it comes to food information the challenges are daunting. Emotional intelligence helps us cope with managing diet and exercise routines that often involve tough choices. We all vary on how well we can cope.

If you feel your own emotional intelligence regarding your personal relationship with food and fitness is not up to the task—seek the support of strong, more emotionally intelligent persons. We often come to know these people as our coaches, personal trainers, and good friends. If we want to become a community of physically fit, mentally active, and emotionally comfortable people, we might as well accept that we're all in this together. Share the load and the weight will come off. We all want to feel good about eating well.

"The mind can deal with limitless information. It handles information emotionally."

~ Howard Nations

"Doing more with less is not to do nothing. Yet doing nothing is the crux of a Zen experience for it brings forth being with more. How so? I do not know."

~ JAL

17

Joyful Moves

There is no quick fix to health. Exercise is not easy regardless of what you see on television or read in a supermarket tabloid. The natural laws of the human body say only one thing, a human has to burn more fuel than it consumes. Burn more calories and fat melts away. Here's how a body knows when enough is enough and too much is an extra chin.

Burn Baby, Burn

Metabolism (we discussed this earlier) is the pilot light for the body's furnace. It's ready to kick in and burn fuel. This ignites with a quick flash of glycogen stored in the muscles and then fat is converted and roasted into glycogen. This keeps the energy supply burning. Exercise keeps your pilot light burning high.

Think of a gas log fireplace where a tiny blue flame is always burning off minute amounts of gas which if not burnt off would be deadly. During summer when warm climate prevails many folks turn off the gas completely and the fire pit is essentially stone, cold, dead.

People who no longer use their bodies, or use them minimally, don't need energy and the pilot light burns lower and lower. Of course, we're not morticians so let's focus on live bodies that need to boost the pilot light and ignite the fire.

Minimal movement resets the metabolism to "ultra low." There is not enough energy to ignite the fuel into a full burn. All that can't be burned is stored as fat. Eventually, fat accumulates to the untenable point where people become plump, rotund, corpulent, overweight, and obese.

Imagine so much left over fuel converted to waste that there isn't enough storage space in the midriff or thighs so the heart and blood system are cohered as additional storage facilities. After awhile the fat colonies begin to take over the vascular walls in the form of cholesterol. Overweight and obesity status is not all about fat. Genetics, environment, behavior, and stress all contribute to body weight. When we obsess about fat we forget about the other factors and lose a holistic view of our lives.

Think instead about the recommendations provided by your doctor during you recent visit. Do you need to lower your blood pressure? Is your cholesterol at dangerous levels? Did you fill any prescriptions? Are you taking your medication as prescribed? Take responsibility for your health and join forces in this wellness campaign.

Start by eating right—that means choosing good foods that are enjoyable and satisfying. Next, focus on exercise and the fitness will follow.

Today is the Past's Future

Health histories are critical to medical diagnostic practices. Draw a family tree in your journal noting the types of diseases that your parents, grandparents and siblings encountered. Given the choice, would you avoid any of these? Circle the illnesses they endured and then ask your self whether diet and fitness could have in any way contributed to the extent of those illnesses.

Reflect on your current health status. Do any of your daily realities seem linked to familiar histories? Sure, so you drag yourself into a gym. Plod over to the treadmill and start walking. Next, move on to the exercise circuit then leave a little sweaty. Be grateful the torture is over. Then you go back two days later and subject yourself to the same routine.

You may notice a little stiffness in your muscles, some slight pain, and think this means you have to lay off for a while. Wrong! That's the bad stuff being exiled from your body. Keep moving your body. Stretching is imperative. Get back into the gym.

The changes happen differently in every body but every body changes. Pay attention to how you feel and acknowledge those changes. Don't be an exercise grouch. Embrace this "right here right now" opportunity to live a longer and more productive life. No whining!

Beautiful Moves

Exercise improves blood flow to all of the mind-body including the biggest organ—your skin. You don't always need to have sex or unprotected sun exposure to have a rosy complexion. Researchers found that people associate pink cheeks with handsome men and beautiful women. The improved blood flow that comes from regular exercise speeds up the healing of zits and encourages skin cell renewal. The beauty of exercise is seen as fewer sags and wrinkles. This refreshed, vibrant look is sure to set a twinkle in your eyes.

Give Notice

Change your perception of exercising. As you begin to note changes in your strength, endurance and wellbeing, you'll also note more positive elements of the world. As you change within, the world changes around you. You are able to do more and enjoy doing. Track these changes in your log. Take a moment to experience gratitude for these changes even if it only means being glad you aren't bedridden and unable to change.

At first you might notice that you're not as breathless, maybe you can tie your shoes more easily, or your body's aches and pains are subsiding.

This might be hard for some of you, but bear with us. We want you to have a true picture of your body image. Remove all clothing and stand in a well-lit room. You are not allowed to be critical of yourself. Fitness starts with loving yourself as you are! In the privacy of your room, look into a mirror and see how well you know the person staring back at you.

Is this the body you remembered from years ago? Does this body look like it's going to be around for the long run? In the Appendix you'll find the **Taking a Closer Look** worksheet. Write your comments there. You can write one word or a paragraph. Be sure to note all the little things about yourself.

Things many come to accept as "old age" may be fitness related such as stiffness and soreness in your arches when you get up in the morning. What about other aches and joint pains? Do you see excess baggage? Where are the bulges on your body and how big are they? Karen had a client whose abdomen hung down and touched the top of her thighs. The day she got out of the shower and realized she could see the tops of her legs she was elated!

If you don't take the time to notice where you are, you won't notices any changes or feel a sense of satisfaction that is the ultimate reward for hard work. You won't keep going forward if you can't recognize how far you have come and how much you left behind.

Once you've written everything you can about how you look and feel as you look at your reflection, go on to the next page and write your long and short term goals. For those of you who are brave enough, take pictures to document your starts; wearing underwear is okay for posterity.

Later we'll discuss types of exercises that combine aerobic activity that kicks up your heart rate and gets your blood humming. You'll learn about smooth moves using resistance to strengthen muscles. Karen will help you design workouts that coordinate in ways that turn on your brain and blow off the fat.

"The recipe for living is to simply do what we're doing. Don't be self-conscious about it, Just do it."

~ C. Joka Beck

"Don't worry about what you can't control. Let's only talk about what you can do."

~ JAL's Dad, Joe Christiano

18

Choosing a Gym

"Three important life decisions are: where to live, what to do, and with whom to do it."

~ *Daniel Gilbert,*
Stumbling on Happiness

Choosing a gym can be a tricky quest, since it represents three caveats for happiness; where, what, and with whom to conduct your fitness training. There is a surplus of fitness venues in many communities. This means many choices and, at the same time, the possibility of dealing with high-pressure sales pitches and promotional opportunities. Fitness centers and gym staff members are trained as sales reps whose job is to boost membership. Lonely? They'll become your best friend. Think nobody's interested in your life? They'll show interest in your family, your habits, and your goals. Worried nobody really cares whether you're thick or thin? It's their job to get to know you and then overcome your objections so you join right away. One of many scenarios goes like this:

"Let's get you started today, Mickey."

"I didn't come to sign up today. I'm just looking."

"Didn't you just say your doctor told you your blood pressure was too high and you need to exercise?"

"Yeah, well…"

"Mickey, there isn't any reason not to get started right now."

Sales are sales. Gyms count on you signing up under pressure or on impulse. The push is necessary to motivate some people. Journal this question, "What's the difference between an impulse and a motivated purchase?" Rather than portend to see the future, don't sign a monthly contract based on that futuristic vision of who you could become. Be realistic—sign on to the contract that meets you in the present and will provide guidance in reasonable steps.

Be concerned if you feel pressured into joining a gym. The trainer may make bold promises about how you will achieve your ideal body with relatively minor life changes. Take a little bit more time to set up the dance before becoming fitness partners. Make informed decisions based on *your* personal motivation. Let the sales rep know you are stacking them up against their competition. Be clear that you have high standards regarding the center's location, parking, cleanliness, environment/equipment, sound system, scent, and taste. Ask if you can do a free week membership to see whether the staff can deliver on its promises. Consider the location, parking, cleanliness, environment, equipment, sound system, scent, taste, and instruction offered by any fitness center you consider joining.

Location

Is the facility within ten minute drive from your home or work? If it's further away your chances of exercising regularly will diminish drastically.

Parking

Parking might sound like it isn't important, but be assured, it is. Avoid a choice that comes packaged with an easy excuse to skip a day. Limited or distant parking affords the "my dog ate my homework" excuse for rainy, snowy, too cold or too hot days. Don't give yourself that option. Make sure there's plenty of parking.

Cleanliness

A gym should be concerned with providing the cleanest possible environment for its members. Top of the line facilities provide small fresh workout towels for their members. Although it is an expense for the facility, it is a perk that sets an "A" club above the others. Members shouldn't have to sit on a piece of equipment and find themselves in someone else's sweat. Some fitness clubs will insist each member bring their own towel. That's better than nothing, but why not go for the free clean towels?

Once you have made your observations ask the staff about its cleaning schedule. The gym should be cleaned once a day. Peek behind the bathroom door to see whether of not a cleaning schedule with time and staff initials is posted. A lot of bodies sweat in a gym throughout the day. Cleaning is the only way to limit the bacteria and viruses that collect on handles and cushions.

Look carefully at the facility. Are the equipment metal frames dusty and dirty? Is the upholstery torn or dull looking from dried sweat? Is there dust under the equipment? Are the showers and bathrooms clean? During the time you are in the facility, do you see members or fitness staff, wiping down equipment? Do they have containers of hand sanitizer around the facility for the members to use?

Equipment

Are there group classes? When they are scheduled, is there room for individuals to work out on weights and use the cardio-equipment? Are there ample treadmills in good working order with options such as video screens, audio-plugs and incline features? Is the facility overcrowded with machines or limited in the types of equipment for upper, lower and core body workouts?

Sound System

Most facilities play music over the loudspeakers, and the music genre you prefer might not be in play. If hip-hop is blaring and you prefer oldie somewhat moldy (Classic Rock) decide whether you'll compensate with an MP3 player or ...learn to tolerate, or even enjoy, their playlists.

Are there loud conversations transacting over the machine noise? Do you find these interesting or distracting? Do people intrude on your concentration during a set repetition?

Is it too quiet with no noise, no friendly banter, and really soft quiet music? Are you confused as to whether you should meditate or sweat?

Scent

Does the gym smell somewhat human without a cleaning fluid odor? There is a balance between a junior high gym locker room stocked with daily-worn six-month-old t-shirts and socks and the antiseptic aroma of a surgical operating room. A clean gym smells fresh despite people burning their own fat and toiling to build muscles.

Taste

Nourishment is essential for a healthy workout. What you choose to eat and drink afterwards should be refreshing and delightful.

Fitness centers usually offer protein drinks made fresh, fruit smoothies, bottled water, and protein bars (they charge for these). Some facilities also offer commercial meal plans to orient people to healthy diets with minimal preparation.

Instruction

Novices! Heads Up! Those machines can hurt if misused! At minimum, a gym should provide an equipment orientation as the first, mandatory introduction to your signed membership. Some facilities give new members free personal training sessions to kick start their program. Don't think of this service as a personal favor. It's in their best interest to have you understand how to use the equipment. It reduces the chance of injury. Fitness centers are interested in your success, and these initial training sessions help point you in the proper direction to succeed so you will tell your friends.

Remember that fitness centers are interested in your success. Look for a certified, educated fitness staff. See if their credentials are posted with valid dates. They should also be trained in Red Cross CPR/AED and First Aid. Staff should be well versed in training techniques for a diverse number of people. Fitness consultants won't do the work for you; rather they should be willing to correct your form or show you an exercise.

If you have special problems (knees, back, shoulder troubles) make sure they have ample experience working with these specialized conditions and are prepared to steer you toward helpful exercises. Don't let staff disregard the very issues that motivated you to sign a contract for their services.

Having bad knees doesn't mean ignore your leg workout. Staff should help you to adjust to exercises that strengthen leg muscles and balance those joints. An exemplary fitness staff helps every member to develop individual programs. If the entire gym is doing the same exercise routine then you should move on to another facility.

Members

Never judge people by their outward appearance. However, if the gym is full of people from another generation you may want to keep looking. Some gyms are social and have their own sense of community. Thinking of emotional intelligence and people's need to bond with others sharing common goals, a fitness center is probably a better environment than a bar. You, however, may not be looking for the Cheers of the fitness world and may be uncomfortable in a "gym rat" social arena.

Ask about peak times and how many members are in the facility, especially during the times you plan on being there. If it's common for 40 members to be present at those times and there are only 10 cardiovascular exercise machines, plan on doing a lot of waiting for the equipment. If you don't know how to use that equipment, staff can show you a treadmill or bike. There are also many exercises that use free weights, balance, and stretching. Go for a week and use different pieces of equipment and watch the people who use it.

Ask other members their opinion of the facility. Clients are the most valid references for any fitness center. Of course they are likely to be positively biased because that's the place they've chosen to center their own fitness program. A big lesson you'll learn is that a seemingly hefty matron may well be able to zap off 10 minutes full bore on the elliptical when you are flushed and breathless after just two!

Like healthy children, adults should be able to play actively. Adult playgrounds, known as gyms or fitness centers, can involve people balancing on great big beach balls, holding 8 lb. weighted balls while moving from squat to standing, lifting a metal rod balanced with a couple of hundred of pounds above the chest, or twisting far to the right and back far to the left with a simple broomstick held with two hands behind the neck. It's fun! And unlike childish playground games, all of the losers are winners!

It's common to forge a solid bond with one or more of the trainers because you can sense their empathy and support for your goals. Physical workouts in a healthy, pleasing and comfortable environment will ground and inspire you. Expect to be able to share with other clients and trainers the remarkable and positive transitions that signal you are becoming closer to that vision of a fit and healthy self.

Choose a gym. Go to the gym. Where ever you go—change will follow. Everything will change because you go, including you. You will notice subtle and profound changes that follow and, you may ask, where does it go? The answer—it goes because of and with you. Pay attention when you go to what goes—and know you are going towards your goal.

19

Exercise for Baby Boomers

The generation born from 1946 to 1964 first made its mark urging the country to "Make Love Not War." The year 2012 heralded the year millions upon millions (think ten thousand per day for the next 19 years!) of these once upon a time revolutionaries begin the rush toward retirement. Yep, back when they were kids they warned each other never to trust anyone over 30—today, they are really concerned whether the kids under 30 are going to take care of them in their twilight years. Why, even their musical icon Jimmy Buffett chides that now they decline tequila for carrot juice.

Rock On

Well, the Boomers certainly partied hearty and now have to pay the proverbial piper. Rather than being "the people our parents warned us about," they are looking a lot like their own grand-parents amid worries about diabetes, high blood pressure, erectile dysfunction, and bad teeth. Getting old isn't for sissies.

Contrary to popular belief, exercise is not for the young alone. Actually, the blunt reality of the American childhood obesity crisis is that exercise is the missing ingredient in 21st century child's play. The day seasoned adults believe they are too old for exercise is the day they can officially retire from living and order a subscription to Modern Immaturity.

Exercise is the cornerstone for senior health. It reduces osteoporosis, heart disease, diabetes, obesity and strokes. Fortunately the benefits don't stop there. Having the stamina to lunch with friends and watch grandchildren play soccer is a pretty good benefit! Maintaining a healthy body with full range of motion in hips and shoulders, and a straight healthy back is a goal to strive for and achieve.

From Soda Jerk to Gym Rat

Ever since Fonzi jumped the shark[32] and laid to rest our fascination with the mid 20th century lives of teenagers, Baby Boomers have sought to make their own mark on the world. Seniors can find the fountain of youth at their local gym, usually in the form of a bottle of water thirstily drank after a brisk workout. Be advised, not all gyms are senior friendly. The science of geriatric exercise is a specific field for physical trainers. Many trainers are oriented toward working with younger athletic clients rather than more age-enhanced members.

When scouting out a gym, ask the staff if their trainers have experience and education with "Special Populations", specifically Senior Exercise. Those trainers can recommend a workout routine specific to your needs and health condition. Approval from your physician is mandatory. The best trainers are open to interfacing with doctors in planning personal fitness and nutrition programs.

---

32 Take a break and have a laugh—watch a snippet of the episode of *Happy Days* at http://www.youtube.com/watch?v=MDthMGtZKa4

The best gyms for seniors also provide a Registered Dietician (RD) for consultation to insure proper nutrition. In lieu of an RD, find a trainer with experience helping people perfect their eating without getting all trendy. While healthy nutrition is an important feature for all gym members, it is particularly important for the Boomers and their elders. Those who cross the centennial divide have physical concerns that are not common to young and middle aged clients.

This Time is Prime

Golden Boomers, welcome to "Prime Time". This is the phase of life Dr. Bill Sears[33], one of the country's best-known family physicians, and his wife Martha define as the second half of life. Baby Boomers are well into their second 50 years as we write this book. They experience daily the general effects of chronological advancement, otherwise known as aging. Their bodies are changing almost as rapidly as their young grandkids'. Dr. Sears has simple advice for Prime Timers to ensure healthy aging, "Keep the sticky stuff out of your body, strengthen your garbage-disposal system, move, and laugh often." This is a great recipe for living well and living long. After all, it's late afternoon in the Age of Aquarius.

Eating well and getting regular physical exercise are essential for maintaining good health during your prime time years. We share the sense that through exercise and good eating it's time to grab the brass ring and celebrate. The good life asks in return that you restore and preserve good health. What is Sears' predication about a generation entering into an uncertain economic era? Too many will focus on saving money, rather than saving their bodies. Remember seniors, paying 20% of a $100,000 medical emergency

33 Read BIll (MD) and Martha Sears' (RN) book on feeling young and living longer, *Prime Time Health* (2009)

means taking $20,000 out of retirement savings (unless there is supplemental insurance).

If the crisis was precipitated by an unhealthy, sedentary lifestyle how much was actually saved by not joining a fitness center? And to all who prevent astronomical levels of health care needs with regular fitness and good nutrition—those gym payments constitute a savvy investment with a national benefit. Save your body by eating right and hitting the gym and you'll have enough cash in your pocket to live it up for a long time.

20

Reflections

About half of the human brain deals with vision. The reflection in our mirrors affects how we feel. How we feel impacts our chances for personal and professional success. When we look and feel our best when our mind-bodies are balanced and healthy.

I Be Me

Over the course of our lifetime we create many self-concepts that define for each an identify of "me." We change our names, social media status, zip codes, jobs, and social circles. We swap and arrange these bits of "me" and become who we imagine ourselves to be at a given moment. "I'm a good son" morphs into "I'm a great Dad." "I'm a runner." "I'm overweight." "I can't get it right."

During the '60s the manufacturer of feminine products Kimberley Clark, had a cartoon ad campaign for teens, "I knew who I was when I woke up this morning. But I've changed since then." The implication is obvious—girls become women. Our lives are but one brief moment in the universe. Who you are at this moment will not necessarily the you of the future.

When we were kids, eating right meant being a member of Mom's "Clean Plate Club." Eating every last morsel of food was mandatory no matter how long it sat forlornly on the plate and was an abomination to a kid's palate. Believing that a healthy appetite for a growing child meant eating increasing quantities of food worked for our parents. After all, they learned about real hunger during the Great Depression. As mid-life adults, many Boomers get depressed, as their "Club Fed" membership becomes evident by their expanding reflection in the mirror.

What worked for Boomers when they were kids causes many to suffer by middle age. This calls for heavy lifting of our Emotional Intelligence. We have to let go of self-images of the long ago active, healthy kids who pleased their parents by eating everything put out on the dinner table. As mindful adults we have to reflect on who the person we see in our mirror is at this very moment.

Look at your observations you wrote on the **Taking a Closer Look** worksheet, and make note of the changes. Don't forget to date your entry because later when you want more body change you will be able approximate the time it will take to reach a new goal. Timing progress motivates persistence.

Chasing change is a time intensive process. If you are one among many who is fighting a lifetime of bad habits and a body paralyzed in the mire of physical addictions—restoring health and building a healthy lifestyle is a long term commitment. Vow to yourself, "I do!" and plan a lifestyle for a lifetime. Be patient with yourself. The Zen of Weight loss is a commitment to moving, thinking, and eating within a good life. Do this and you will achieve a new, higher standard of living well.

Weighing Anchors

Karen proposes you throw away the scale. Jeri disagrees. She uses it as a tool for "constant vigilance" with a weekly check in routine. She notes its variance up and down and connects the changes with subtle differences in her diet and exercise during the previous week. Some people need to measure inches or pounds on a regular basis. It becomes a fixture of their fitness program. These approaches are different, but they reflect Karen's koan to be keenly aware of your body's status.

We recommend a self-valuation process like simply looking in the mirror. It is quite all right to become somewhat narcissistic. Spending time reflecting on your reflection can be a healthy way to keep track of your weight loss. This will backfire if you are a harsh critic of your own body. Remember that at 50 or 60 your body cannot look as it did when you were 20. Be the best you can be and celebrate life's changes.

Self-valuation of a successful weight loss plan includes heightened awareness of simply feeling good. Fresh thoughts about enhanced energy, sustained inner-peace and a robust approach to life are positive results. In your head—you are becoming lighter!

Avoid being complacent and ambivalent with an overweight form. You are not stuck with that body. Love it by moving it about; feeding and watering it like a prized hothouse orchid.

However, if you are eating well, rarely cheating, and exercising you may still find your legs are bigger than you would like. Now comes the point where you decide on adopting a fitness level that can be comfortably maintained. We will discuss this in the next section.

*"He who has a why to live
can bear almost any how."*

~ Fredrich Nietzsche

*"When I breathe deep –
I move on."*

~ JAL

Zen of Health Promotion

21

Let's set up a plan. You've decided to adopt The ZWL for yourself but question how to fit fitness into your schedule. Can you hear the litany of excuses? The standard grade school excuse, "the dog ate my homework" has evolved to new heights. Deeply emotional reasons for slacking off your exercise and fitness routine are camouflaged excuses. These differ from painful physical feelings, or sensations that signal body injury. When the body signals, "Holy crapola this isn't just muscle burn it's serious pain!" it's time to modify the plan.

Pay attention; talk with your trainer or physician about adjusting The ZWL routine. Self-doubting one's own inner strength in lieu of priority commitments to children, spouse, or job are self-esteem issues. Doubt masks dark feelings of being less meaningful to others than they are to you. Those reasons don't cut it.

Excuse Me

What's the purpose of an excuse? It's an attempt to get off the hook by justifying or overlooking a shortcoming or obligation. Let's take a look at the granddaddy of excuses; "I don't have the time." The recommended exercise time is a minimum of 30-minutes a day, although recent studies suggest this is only a starting point and our bodies really need more.

Start here: elevate your heart rate for 30 minutes or longer and you'll begin to experience some benefit. Exercise puts a spring back in your step, lowers blood pressure and cholesterol, and fights off diabetes with a little extra work. Choosing not to exercise actually exercises the choice to tempt disease and illness.

Excuses are not great supporters of self-esteem, mindfulness, or fitness. You aren't thinking right when you try to exonerate yourself from health! Who in their right mind takes flight from health or embraces illness? The mature way to handle health promotion is to accept that daily exercise is as much a routine as brushing your teeth.

A dear friend in Virginia had a very different lifestyle than Karen's. She was a massage therapist dedicated to the earth religions. She embodied a free-spirit approach to life. She was a beautiful mother of two wonderful children. She didn't go to doctors, instead optioning for a homeopathic approach to health and fitness. Generally, a homeopathic approach complements disease treatment systems (i.e., traditional western medicine). To complement a system doesn't mean to ignore all of its practices. Conversely, she didn't exercise or keep track of her body. When her breast cancer was diagnosed, it was already Stage III. She fought a valiant fight that ended 18 months later.

Could she have warded off death had she had been in touch with her body? If she had been diagnosed earlier would it have made a difference in treatment options and the prognosis? Nobody knows. Statistics suggest that regular mammograms and self-exams decrease mortality from breast cancer. The tragedy is that she didn't keep up with her body and it got away from her. Fitness lends itself to being in touch with your physical self.

Just about everybody gets sick at one time or another. People who are fit are likely to get sick less often. When illness tags people in "good shape" they have more physical, mental, and emotional resources to fight back and are apt to heal quicker.

The Surgeon General advocates regular exercise as a core strategy for becoming a "Healthy and Fit Nation" (2010)[34]. The report is blunt, "Today's epidemic of overweight and obesity threatens the historic progress we have made in increasing American's quality and years of healthy life." The facts are irrefutable; extra pounds hurt the body and shorten the prospect of living long and prosperously. People who exercise have a much lower risk of ever having to face many illnesses on the nation's menu of health crises. That said, the report goes on to state that, "Americans need to live and work in places that help them practice healthy behaviors." The Zen of Weight Loss is *health promotion*.

But what if, just for a moment, time is a barrier to a successful fitness routine? Journal about the time not spent working out, grabbing quick bites at the convenience store after pumping gas, and whatever took place during your regular time at the gym. Pick a few choice words that best describe the reflection in the morning mirror and the body state that finally hits the pillow each night. Are you moving towards or away from your goal?

Watch Dogs

Making time for daily exercise is a bit like having two watchdogs named Timex and Rolex. Your love is whole-hearted and you can trust the results. The list of excuses can be rather lengthy, but here are a few rebuttals:

- No money? Try cutting out one soda a day, at $1.50 each. That saves $45 a month. Many gym memberships can be had for less than $40 a month. Work with the staff about the sign-up fee. That amount is always negotiable. Just keep talking, if the staff balks, move on to another gym willing to waive or reduce the fee.

- Don't know how to do exercises? You may need to pay for an initial orientation and workout plan but after that you can be on your own. Ask the staff to give you a tour and explain what each machine does for body fitness. Try a free group intro lesson to see whether group workouts fit your style. If you don't feel a good fit with staff and other clients, find another gym.

- Embarrassed to be there in revealing clothes? Then don't wear clothes that make you uncomfortable, select loose fitting shirts and pants that cover your body.

- Too many candles on your cake? On the wrong side of the centennial divide? Sorry Dear Heart, but health promotion and disease prevention are two concepts being championed by many Baby Boomers! It's never too late to begin to exercise. Lots of Karen's clients are in their 70s and 80s. Why tempt fate? Stay on top of your game and buy into fitness.

Eliminate excuses. Don't enable failure—accentuate success. Set a positive tone for your body, mind, and emotions to thrive. Excuses are part of a failed defense system. They give power to irrational reasons for not protecting healthy defenses, such as daily exercise and a moderate diet, from functioning.

Rationalize each achievement—five extra minutes on the elliptical or letting out an extra notch of the belt—as the product of your focus, wise eating choices, and pure sweat from an exhilarating workout. Focus on the positive image of the healthy state of wellbeing you strive to achieve. Own your effort, habits, and persuasions relative to fitness. Be one with your personal health and wellbeing goals. Go forward.

Michael: I don't know anyone who could get through the day without two or three juicy rationalizations. They're more important than sex.

Sam Weber: Ah, come on. Nothing's more important than sex.

Michael: Oh yeah? Ever gone a week without a rationalization?

~ The Big Chill

"Ration your rationalizations.
Be real."

~ *JAL*

ZWL

"If you cannot find the truth right
where you are, where else do you
expect to find it?"

~ Chuang-tzu

22

Swifter, Higher, Stronger

The motto of the Olympics is, "Cituis, Altius, Fortius." This Latin phrase translates to "swifter, higher, stronger" because it captures the spirit of sports for the joy of sports. Yes, it is also about winner, in terms of ever stretching the limits of physical abilities; understanding how physical activity sharpens the mind and tones the body. This section is designed to help you select one thing to change. Remember to write in your journal. It is an invaluable tool for building mind-body wellness.

The Flow of Movement

Exercise is a form of movement that demands concentration. It can be an intensely pleasurable experience if it is accompanied by a positive attitude. Rather than consider exercise from a negative "gotta" approach, see it as a "wanna". When viewed as a deeply personal choice of how one truly wants to spend time, the mind centers on happiness as the motivation to move the body in a vigorous manner. Conversely, if exercise is approached with the attitude of a freshly condemned prisoner, the mind will find ways to avoid punishing its body.

ZWL frames fitness in the context of optimal experiences where, through exercise, mindfulness, and healthy nutrition you discover greater happiness and a way to extend these feelings for a long time to come. The notion of focusing on the experience of working out, savoring a meal, or the silence within during a meditation is central to our focus on how you move, feel, and think right now. If it is worth changing, then we discuss ways to change today. The future is an abstraction, and you, at this moment, are a concrete being. Our job is not to predict the future; it's to deal with you as you are right now. Even subtle changes have the power to make significant changes in your future.

There are relationships between readers and writers, trainers and clients. The first step Karen's clients take is to simply observe personal eating habits as they begin our fitness training. Few people can make multiple changes at once. There are too many old patterns, emotions, and habits to change when trying to tackle diet and exercise simultaneously. Start with exercise. It is easier to add a pattern than it is to change patterns.

Some people are able to make dietary and exercise changes at once. Many of Karen's clients notice immediate social and physical benefits of the ZWL program. Others are reluctant to take charge on their own. If you backslide and find the ZWL demands to be overwhelming, focus on a more general goal such as, "I want to feel good about myself." You can develop more specific goals later.

Figure out how you will measure your goals—what do you expect to see or feel that will signal whether or not progress is achieved? Concentrate on the goal and pay attention to signs (expected as well as surprises) of change. Change and then focus on change again.

Focus on your goals. What you work to achieve is waiting for you. Allow the body to move in the way it was intended, to function as the instrument God designed. The body and brain will begin to feed off each other. Some of Karen's clients started an exercise program and after two months felt better. Some voluntarily stopped smoking. They were intrinsically motivated. They experienced deep enjoyment and total involvement with life. ZWL is a means of experiencing the joy of flow. A number of smokers grew to hate cigarettes because they couldn't breathe when they were on the treadmill. Other smokers reported that they didn't need cigarettes because they were empowered.

Exercise is not really complicated. There are three primary areas of fitness: Cardio-Respiratory, Flexibility, and Muscular Strength with Endurance. These big three should be incorporated into your weekly schedule.

Cardio-Respiratory

An effective cardio workout must be continuous, steady and challenging for at least 30 minutes per session. Choose one of the following strategies:

walking	treadmill
elliptical trainer	bike
swimming	

Stretching

Stretching for some is a stretch, but it is important to lengthen the muscles and improve circulation and range of motion of the body's joints. Consider joining yoga or Pilates groups or do assisted stretching with a knowledgeable trainer. Stretches need to be held for a long period of time. Stretch after you exercise and time yourself.

Muscular Strength and Endurance

Strength and endurance will allow you to do the things you used to do. This is the one way to raise that pilot light of yours. When you have increased your muscle mass, your body will require more fuel simply to exist. You will burn more calories even while you sleep. It will awaken your body and start the healing process. Join a local gym. Your membership will strengthen your muscles and emotional intelligence. Begin with staff with that will teach you circuit training. Select a gym that offers a complete orientation session where you will be instructed on the use of each machine. Look for trained fitness professionals and a club with a policy of helpfulness and customer service.

Exercises

ZWL provides a general workout routine designed for every individual using this manual. This manual has not written specific exercises because of the enormous assortment of exercises and equipment available in gyms. It is imperative you stick to one program. While social relationships and fitness tend to get better over time, it's not a good idea to listen to side advice from other clients while you are becoming proficient. Don't do an exercise just because you see someone else doing it.

Novices and readers who have not exercised in a long time will want to start with the Beginning Workout and change as indicated in ZWL. If you have some experience training in a gym, you will need to look ahead and select a level most appropriate for your fitness level.

Two terms will be used to describe ZWL exercise routines:

Set: A set represents a block of time spent doing repeated movement. For example; if you are doing 1 set of 15 repetitions of a leg extension (1×15) this means you use the leg extension machine once and raise your legs 15 times in a slow and powerful motion.

Repetitions: The number of times you repeat the movement in a set. This manual has you performing 15 repetitions to build endurance with the muscle strength.

WARNING: This advice assumes you have been given a release from your family physician to exercise. Remember, you are responsible for monitoring how you feel. Taking a heart rate, either through the touch pads on many exercise machines or by using your *Rate of Perceived Exertion* is important for your safety. If at any time you feel light headed or shortness of breath, stop exercising immediately and seek help.

Let's recap The ZWL fitness plan:
- You are exercising.
- You are working out at least three days a week, depending on your beginning fitness level.
- You are keeping a food journal to identify the foods your body likes.

Our theme is that you are an individual who is becoming ever more conscious of your social relationship with food and you are exercising as a means to realize a personal vision of yourself as fit and trim.

Choose to Change

Brains accept exercise as a wonder drug. Exercise sends an optimal daily dose of blood brimming with nutrients, glucose, and oxygen to "feed your head." This fuels the gray matter to make you feel and think well.

Change more than your underwear every day. Change the way you move through life. Play simple sports, hike, walk, swim, and park in the spot furthest from the office door. Enjoy staring at your thoughts and melting away their negative aspects. Learn to recognize thought chains that look endlessly back on themselves like a snake swallowing its tail. You can learn to make bad thoughts disappear like ocean mist after sunrise. You won't miss bad thoughts or hurtful feelings. An old Buddhist saying states, "bad thoughts will find in you only an empty house." You'll have nothing to lose and they will be able to steal nothing from your happiness.

"Ever since happiness heard your name, it has been running through the streets to find you."

~ Hafiz of Persia

"I'm as happy as I can be — and that is a great deal."

~ JAL

23

ZWL Week at a Glimpse

Let's fit exercise into your week. You'll use a variety of resistance equipment to exercise such as cords, stability balls, and dumbbells. The first step is to schedule time for exercise on your calendar. No excuses, it is time to get down to business.

For this explanation you'll start a ZWL routine on Monday. Begin the workweek with an upper body workout. On Wednesday you'll do lower body workout. Friday will be a prep day for the weekend by repeating the body routine. This makes the weekend a sandwich between workouts.

The following week you'll flip the routine and you start the week on Monday with a lower body workout. This is a "heads I win, tails I still win" global approach to fitness training. Your entire body will tone up over the course of each month as you work the northern hemisphere harder one week and the southern hemisphere takes it slower. The situation reverses when the southern hemisphere gets its due and the northern parts go along for the ride. This approach to lifting weight is called Periodization. While used primarily for athletic "peak performance", it works especially well for fitness-lifters by allowing the body the time it needs to recover.

Now that you understand how to schedule training, go ahead and fill in your calendar to suit your lifestyle. You are going to lift, either at the gym or at home, three days a week. Between lifting days you'll do cardio or major movement activities.

The goal is to be in ZWL Movement for six days out of the week. This will give you a great exercise experience without injury.

Set your Schedule and Schedule your Sets!

	Monday	Tuesday	Wednesday	Thursday	Friday	Saturday	Sunday
Week 1	Upper body	Walk in the park	Lower body	Stretching	Upper body	Rest	Sailing
Week 2	Lower body	Stretching	Upper body	Walk the dog	Lower body	Bike ride	Rest

Moderation

Since we've mentioned the risk of injuries, let's touch on how to reduce the risk of strains, rips, tears, moans and groans. Start warming up by simply walking or biking 10–20 minutes. In nice weather it's great to be outdoors. Unless you're reading this in San Diego where the sea breezes are constant and the sun keeps shining, there will be days when there's not enough Gortex in town to protect you from the elements. So stay inside and use the exercise equipment you've been using as a clothes rack. Get moving! Maintain a pace where you're a little breathless but are still able to talk in complete sentences. Gasping for air is a clear signal that you need to walk slower. Try to *keep moving*. As you become more comfortable with walking, increase the length of time and pick up the pace.

When you begin resistance training remember to be practical and conservative. Don't try to do four sets the first day. Be reasonable with the amount of tension you are using on the resistance bands. Start with the lighter dumbbells. Err on the side of caution and avoid injury. Start with just one round of the exercises at first. Stretch after your workout.

Plan on walking, stretching, swimming or biking on the days between workouts. You're establishing a habit when you get to the third day of your new program. Train your brain. Recall our discussions about how much brains appreciate patterns. Reward yourself with longer walks and concentrated bursts of "me time" as your schedule permits. Up to an hour is the recommended length of time for healthy exercise. Be mindful of the importance of burning, blazing neural pathways that keep your metabolism in the left lane on the ZWL.

All the same rules we discussed in the last chapter apply for this workout. Don't get carried away because you think your legs are stronger and more capable. If your legs haven't done this kind of exercise in the past you will feel it. Setting the bar too high simply invites failure and tricks the brain into avoiding future encounters with any exercise routines.

Use the off days to keep in touch with your mind-body. We call these recovery days. Think about recovery in terms of regaining a healthy body, repossessing fitness, and rescuing yourself from the slippery slope of declining strength and agility. Stretching gets the kinks out and keep the joints healthy. Reward your effort in the ZWL with a nice walk during which you take in the sounds of nature rather than Lady Gaga blasting in your ear buds. Enjoy silence in the place behind your eyelids and north of the soles of your feet. It's the ZWL way.

Moderation is the key with any fitness program. If your body is too sore you won't want to continue to exercise. Take the weekend to become more active with your family and friends. Try to walk outside, fly a kite or go to the park and read your book. Communing with nature will give you benefits that reach soul deep.

A final aspect of this program is breathing. It's vital to life and very important in the practice of Zen, it is also important to the foundation of exercise. Let's transition to the next section with a cleansing breath in through the nose, deep into the lungs, and slowly release between your lips.

Breathe

Zen is about breathing, pace, intuition, and becoming aware. As you move against the resistance created by the bands or weights, focus on each breath. You're going to keep breathing whether you focus or not—but focusing on breathing brings mindfulness into play.

Weightlifters are taught to exhale on the exertion. Take a bicep curl as an example of the focus on breath. Exhale as the weight is moved toward the shoulder. Teaching breathing to most newbies is difficult. The bottom line is that the muscle needs oxygen. Lifters should just breathe naturally. It is a much better approach than holding your breath. So, let's remember to breathe full and slow and get as much oxygen into the body and likewise the muscle.

With your lungs full of air you begin to pull the weight toward your shoulder *exhaling* during the lift.

As you start to *inhale* lower the weight to the starting position (elongate the muscle). The exhalation should last for the duration of the movement. If you join a gym, consider asking a staff member to check your technique (the way you perform each exercise) and make sure you are doing it correctly.

Karen's Koans

More is not better. So you lift 10 pounds and your muscle looks good. Imagine if you lifted 20 pounds? You may find your ligaments and or tendons will get tiny little tears in them. That will lead to an injury that can put you on the bench for a while.

"Be here now."

~ Ram Dass

"Breathe deep to where memories keep."

~ JAL

24

Starting to Workout— Level 1

This routine lasts 2-4 weeks depending on your fitness level. Stay with the exercise routine until you see your progress slow or stop. Progress stalls when you've hit a plateau. It means your body is ready to take on more. Don't be discouraged if you need to stay longer at this. Comparing yourself with the standard, or the usual and customary, is the wrong approach. No two people are alike. This is your workout. Tailor it to your fitness level. Be sure to stay with it.

Beginning exercise starts with easy movement. Jumping into a scrum at a weekend rugby match or playing a full game of handball isn't the way to get acclimated to exercise.

Stay Away from the Gumption Gap

Karen has seen that people make steadier progress by getting started in The ZWL with less rigorous initial workouts. Grabbing onto heavier weights or stiff intensity all but guarantee clients wake up the next day feeling unduly sore. The pain doesn't gain much enthusiasm for the next appointment. Avoid going so far past your limits that you fall into the "gumption gap." The gumption gap is a netherland of a weakened mind-set that can be triggered by a nasty event—like a strained ligament. This sets off a negative feedback loop, "exercise leads to pain leads to frustration leads to more pain, so let's not exercise." The gumption gap is where we back off or lose enthusiasm for continuing down the ZWL path. Of course, the less you try the more likely you'll realize less success and sense greater failure. That's a discouraging loop of negative thinking that leads to bad decisions. If you start to think exercise and mindful eating are bad investments, you can't expect a fitness bonus at the end of the quarter.

Split Routines

We recommend the Upper/Lower split routine that we discussed in the last chapter. It looks like this:

Split workout routine

Upper Body	Lower Body
Chest	Legs
Shoulders	Back
Biceps	Triceps
Abdomen	Abdomen

At Level 1 do at least one exercise for each muscle group. Do each exercise for one series (or set) for 15 repetitions. The same thing goes for each of the muscles listed in the chart. You'll determine the specific type of exercise to do by following these guidelines.

Chest. Push-ups, done from any position, is chest exercise. Lying on the floor or a bench then lifting soup cans or a barbell is chest exercise.

Shoulders. Shoulders are best worked by lifting something over your head to put it on a shelf. The stretching and pressing actions of the arms up above the head are what you are working for.

Biceps. The front of the arm can be worked by pulling your hands toward your chest and shoulders from the starting position where they hang loosely by your legs.

Abdominal Exercises. They used to be called sit-ups and crunches. Now they are just known as Abs! This body part is very important and very volatile. Be aware that strain in your back is your body signaling your brain to smarten up and adjust the exercise. Expect to feel soreness in and across the abdomen as the muscles tone up.

Leg. Squatting, lunging and jumping garner their power from leg muscles. Guard your knees carefully—if any types of movement result in a startling pain—give it up.

Back. The lower back is made stronger by a healthy abdominal complex. The strength between your shoulder blades and in the upper back is what gives us good posture.

Triceps. The back of the arm. Triceps tend to develop the annoying habit of continuing to wave even though your hand stopped moving. Karen's clients have a saying, "A day without Triceps exercise is like a day without sunshine!"

Triceps are amazing and can be worked with either straight or bent arms. Just be sure you feel a pinch in the back of the arm that indicates they are working.

Perform each exercise one at a time for fifteen repetitions. Make sure the weight is heavy enough that your muscles feel like you are moving through mud rather than air. The weight should offer a low level of resistance. Don't push each lift so hard that the muscles feel as if they are going burnout before the 15th repetition.

Daily Dose of The ZWL

Level 1 involves baby steps for novices to the fitness world. This initiation to ZWL propels their sense of will towards their goals. Taking tiny sips will still empty the cup and quench the thirst. Level 1 demands an open mind that allows for doubt and possibility for those sensing newness within and around. Done well, Level 1 is when things that were once appeared as normal (Supersize) become strange.

Over the course of a couple weeks, Level 1 is when things that once appeared rare ("Those are MY toes? I can see them as I stand up straight and look down!") become common. Completing Level 1 is a sign that your body is stronger and your resolve to live life mindfully is coming to greater fruition. The changes will continue to amaze and delight you. Move along.

Week 1 at a glimpse

Monday Gym Day	Walk on Treadmill – 20 minutes. If feels too hard, walk slower but *keep moving* for 20 minutes. Some people find that at first 10 minutes is enough. Do Circuit Training Upper Body – 1 set, 15 repetitions. Stretch after your workout.
Tuesday Off	Stretching is a good thing to do today.
Wednesday Gym Day	Walk on Treadmill – 20 minutes. (If it is hard, go slower but *keep moving* for 20 minutes.) Do Circuit Training Lower Body – 1 set, 15 repetitions. Stretch after your workout.
Thursday Off	Stretching is a good thing to do today.
Friday Gym Day	Walk on Treadmill – 20 minutes. (If it is hard, walk slower but *keep moving* for 20 minutes.) Do Circuit Training Upper Body – 1 set, 15 repetitions. Stretch after your workout.
Saturday or Sunday Off	Stretching is a good thing to do today. Take a walk on the other day.

Week 2

Monday	Lower Body
Wednesday	Upper Body
Friday	Lower Body

25

Step Up Your
Workout—Level 2

By now the beginners have been working out for about a month. Their bodies feel better, energy levels have increased and folks are feeling good enough to take it a step further. Let's join up here at Level 2 and spend the next 4 weeks improving fitness a little more. Want to hang out at this level longer? It's your choice. Stay with any exercise routine until you see your progress slow or stop. Know when it's time to step up the program, commit and go!

Now it might be time to check your weight and measurements. If you would rather wait, by all means, wait. Be considerate of the fresh relationship blossoming from The ZWL inner guidance system.

In this next segment we are going to power up on the cardio workout and resistance training. Exercises are done in two sets. An additional 10 minutes of cardio have been added. Also, on the independent walking days, get out for 30 minutes of brisk movement. These are days to stretch your mind as well as your legs.

Level 2 is a healthy ZWL approach that fits most schedules. You might become more capable of working with heavier weights. If that's the case, only increase the weights in five-pound increments for the arm and shoulder exercises. On the larger muscle groups (chest, back and legs) you're probably be safe increasing the weights by 10 pounds.

Pay attention to your proper form and breathing. Above all, don't get distracted by other people's suggestions based on their histories. As they suggest things, politely share that you've figured out what works for you. ZWL encourages you to keep journaling. You have a plan—stick with it. This is your ZWL path. Your brain, mind, and body are moving forward in this very moment of stillness.

ZWL Week at a Glimpse

Week 1

Monday Gym Day	**Warm up** with 20 minutes on the treadmill.
	Circuit Training Upper Body – 2 exercises for each body part. 1st Set, 15 repetitions total. (If 2 exercises are too many, stay with one exercise each muscle group.) Start with the first set: Chest, Shoulders, Biceps and Abs.
	Walk on Treadmill – 3-5 minutes. (If it is hard, go slower but keep moving.)
	Circuit Training Upper Body – 2 exercises for each body part. 2nd Set, 15 repetitions total. (If 2 exercises are too many, stay with one exercise each muscle group.) Start with the first set: Chest, Shoulders, Biceps and Abs.
	Walk on Treadmill – 3-5 minutes.
	Repeat for 3rd Set if you feel like you can do it.
	Cool Down by walking 10 minutes.
	Stretch after your workout.
Tuesday Cardio Day	**Walk** in your neighborhood or go back to the gym and get in at least 30 minutes.

Wednesday Gym Day	Warm up with 20 minutes on the treadmill.
	Circuit Training Lower Body – 2 exercises for each body part. 1st Set, 15 repetitions total. (If 2 exercises are too many, stay with one exercise each muscle group.) Start with the first set: Legs, Back, Triceps and Abs.
	Walk on Treadmill – 3-5 minutes. (If it is hard, go slower but keep moving.)
	Circuit Training Lower Body – 2 exercises for each body part. 2nd Set, 15 repetitions total. (If 2 exercises are too many, stay with one exercise each muscle group.) Start with the first set: Legs, Back, Triceps and Abs.
	Walk on Treadmill – 3-5 minutes.
	Repeat for 3rd Set if you feel like you can do it.
	Cool Down by walking 10 Minutes.
	Stretch after your workout.
Thursday Cardio Day	**Walk** in your neighborhood or go back to the gym and get in at least 30 minutes.
Friday Gym Day	**Warm up** with 20 minutes on the treadmill.
	Circuit Training Upper Body – 2 exercises for each body part. 1st Set, 15 repetitions total. (If 2 exercises are too many, stay with one exercise each muscle group.) Start with the first set: Chest, Shoulders, Biceps and Abs.
	Walk on Treadmill – 3-5 minutes. (If it is hard, go slower but keep moving.)
	Circuit Training Upper Body – 2 exercises for each body part. 2nd Set, 15 repetitions total. (If 2 exercises are too many, stay with one exercise each muscle group.) Start with the first set: Chest, Shoulders, Biceps and Abs.
	Walk on Treadmill – 3-5 minutes.
	Repeat for 3rd Set if you feel like you can do it.
	Cool Down by walking 10 Minutes.
	Stretch after your workout.
Saturday or Sunday Cardio Day	**Walk** in your neighborhood or go back to the gym and get in at least 30 minutes.

Week 2

Monday	Lower Body
Wednesday	Upper Body
Friday	Lower Body

26

Fit Enough to Do More—Level 3

The Level 3 routine can occur after about six to eight weeks of concentrated focus on The ZWL. By this point you have earned the right to be called a "Gym Rat". That is a term of endearment used for Karen's clients who start a program and stick with it.

Be proud of yourself. You have overcome a myriad of excuses that kept you hot glued to the desk, waist deep in the couch potato patch, and away from the gym and fitness. Working out is a lifestyle commitment that must be something your mind-body can sustain for a long time. Even geriatric facilities have regular exercise programs. Residents might only bounce balloons back and forth in their wheel chairs, but the concentration on movement keeps them tethered to the moment. Consider augmenting your exercises to be sure to avoid overtraining or overuse injuries. We'll provide some alternatives at the end of this chapter.

ZWL workouts for Level 3 include rigorous practice of at least one exercise for each of the muscle groups/body parts. Your brain is sending millions of messages through well-greased pathways to the chest, legs, back, shoulders, biceps, triceps and abs! It's a whole new level of intense fitness designed to keep your metabolism fired up, mind expanding, and spirits elevated.

Week at a glimpse

Monday Gym Day	**Circuit Training Whole Body** – 3 sets, 15 repetitions. **Walk on Treadmill** – 30 minutes. (If it is hard, go slower but *keep moving* for 30 minutes.) **Stretch** after your workout.
Tuesday Cardio Day	Walk in your neighborhood or go back to the gym and get in at least 30 minutes.
Wednesday Gym Day	**Circuit Training Whole Body** – 3 sets, 15 repetitions. **Walk on Treadmill** – 30 minutes. (If it is hard, go slower but *keep moving* for 30 minutes.) **Stretch** after your workout.
Thursday Cardio Day	Walk in your neighborhood or go back to the gym and get in at least 30 minutes.
Friday Gym Day	**Circuit Training Whole Body** – 3 sets, 15 repetitions. **Walk on Treadmill** – 30 minutes. (If it is hard, go slower but *keep moving* for 30 minutes.) **Stretch** after your workout.
Saturday or Sunday Cardio Day	Walk in your neighborhood or go back to the gym and get in at least 30 minutes.

Here are the different ways you can switch out the Level 3 routine.

- Do the exercises more slowly and with less resistance/weight.

- Static work is always helpful for the muscles. Pause mid-motion to keep the stress on the muscle and take it off the joint. Hold the position for about for a count of 15 to 30 seconds.

- Instead of 15 repetitions try slightly heavier weights and do 10–12 reps.

- Make sure not to do the same exercise for each body part. Brains love surprises as well as routines. If you have been doing a chest press machine for your chest, try to do dumbbell bench press instead. The change-up will stoke the metabolism just as a curve ball snaps the batter's attention.

- You can always go back to a Level 1 or Level 2 for a day if you have a time crunch. The rule is—avoid paying half-hearted attention to the schedule. The current of a falling stream is much stronger than a swimmer's upstream strokes. It's much harder to get started again.

- Know your limits.

Part of baseball folklore is that the famous NY Yankees catcher Yogi Berra understood and accepted that he could never be a pitcher. Why? Because, as he put it, he had an awkward motion— every time he brought his left arm forward he hit himself in the ear. By the end of Level 3 you know what your body can and can't withstand. You've learned when to expect a second wind. There are days when you step on the elliptical, slip on the iPod and know that nothing, simply nothing comes, between you and the sense that your whole mind-body is in sync. Awkward motions are supplanted by smooth, satisfying routines that bring about a good sweat and a deep sense of accomplishment.

Level 3 is at the pinnacle of The ZWL fitness training. This is when what's been taught about fitness is converted to exercise, diet, and wellbeing. You successfully practice lessons learned and thus are enlightened by mindful fitness.

Perhaps you began Level 1 hoping you'd have an answer to why all the other people in the gym seemed to move stronger and longer than you could. Rather than fight and resist change, you've learned to deal with it. You're embracing changes reflected in the mirror such as a tighter tush. Now you know that you can and do have the inner strength to push your own limits. You moved and the world changed.

Personal Trainers

The emphasis of The ZWL is for you to make the choices about your own health, weight, and fitness. With this chapter we are not suggesting another route, but rather trying to show you the benefits of integrating professional guidance in your program.

Some people consider a personal trainer as a luxury. Others find that a weekly appointment with their trainer is essential for keeping with the program. Working with the trainer becomes a formal commitment that sharpens your focus and accelerates progress. It sustains your innate desire to thrive. Here are a few good reasons for using a personal trainer:

- **Education.** A personal trainer will help you set up your exercise routine based on the results you want to achieve. Besides that, this individual can keep you from getting injured by teaching proper technique.

- **Technique and Form.** Even the most experienced lifter can break form and do poor technique. A personal trainer constantly checks the biomechanics of your body to ensure you will be working proper muscles in the correct way. They will also make sure you are doing the right exercises for the right body parts. Karen has had people performing a back exercise on their chest day. It's nice to have someone who checks you all the time.

- **Special Populations.** This group of the public is steadily growing as we Baby Boomers begin to reap the rewards of our past injuries. People who have heart disease, stroke, old injuries, Parkinsons, etc., can benefit from a person trained in this area. Karen's certification in Post Rehabilitation Exercise has prepared her to work with along with physicians to keep bodies strong. Strength means less likelihood of falling.

- **Sports specific training.** Want help with your golf swing? You may need the benefit of a personal trainer along with your golf pro. Any pro or college team in the nation can tell you the benefits of having a trainer on staff. A Sports Specific trainer can help you too. Be sure she or he is experienced in the sport you are training for.

- **Bored or Hitting a Brick Wall.** Tired at the end of the day? Think you might skip out? Personal trainers offer accountability and motivation. Rarely do trainers find a client who is willing to throw away their money because they blow off a session. The advantage of having a trainer at the gym can be the difference between seeing progressive results with no injury. You may hit a point after several months of training when you see your results stall. Often it is time to spice up your current program and a trainer can make adjustments so you don't have to do the same rote exercises. There is nothing worse than being bored. You will stop coming altogether.

Consider your first day in a gym. If you have no prior experience, trainers may appear to be speaking another language. You probably don't know a chest press from a leg press. You need a roadmap to this new world and the way to get it is with a personal trainer. Personal training is available in several packages. When signing up at our gym new members are encouraged to purchase a three-session Personal Training package. It's not realistic to think you'll get the benefit of everything that trainer knows in one session. Karen writes a program for each new client based on his or her physical status and fitness goals.

Additional packages are available everywhere. Your pocketbook will determine what you will be able to do. In a perfect world you would be able to see a trainer three days a week for a few months. While it has always been difficult to think about paying for luxuries in life, we will always find a way to compromise. You will find a way that works for you. There are choices that can be affordable.

Karen's Koans

Not all trainers are created equal. Make sure the person you are hiring is qualified with a recognized agency. You may be fortunate enough to find someone with additional education as a physical therapist. Ask them to discuss the limitations you might have due to previous injuries. They should be willing to speak with you.

Several of Karen's clients elect to work with her once a week. She outlines the training they will do on their own and then monitors them while she raises the bar and checks their progress with one-on-one training weekly. During Karen's sessions with clients she weighs, measures, and charts improvement. Progress is palpable, tangible, and obvious. There are significant and lasting changes in your body, wellbeing, and fitness level.

Probably one of the most popular forms of personal training is group training or boot camps. Class sizes vary and usually meet twice a week. It's a program designed to give you the personal training experience on a budget. It's vastly popular as members generate great results in terms of muscles built, fat lost, slimmer hips, and big grins.

Trainers tune into each client's individual needs that change over time. Is it time to get ready for ski season? The training routine builds leg strength, flexibility, and stamina. Do you have a special social event on the calendar that you want to wear a strapless gown or sundress? The routine shifts to working on the quadriceps and upper arms. Karen calls this body sculpting. She concentrates resistance training and weight lifting on particular body parts that shape you towards your goal.

A personal trainer is your private motivator and cheering squad who designs and manages the fitness program. The professional nature of the arrangement—you're paying for this time and attention—adds accountability to your fitness commitment. A trainer is your personal coach and friend. Karen has a client who does ongoing training. Once they established the routine and did several training sessions together, the client carried on independently. She follows the workouts Karen prescribes and when she has questions or concerns or is just ready for some changes she says, "Hey Karen, I want to hire you to be my best friend!" They set up a personal training session for the next day. Hire yourself a "best friend" and get the boost you need to find your results.

Select a Personal Trainer

The National Board of Fitness Educators (NBFE) reports the average hourly rate for a trainer is $60-70 per session depending on your geographical location. Our facility presently charges $50 per session and with a package the price drops ten dollars per session. This same organization maintains a list of reputable certification agencies.

The first thing you want to look into is the training of the person you elect to coach you. You can download the listing from the NBFE web site.[35] Karen holds two certifications with one of the agencies accredited by the NBFE.

Karen's training is through the American Fitness Professionals and Associates (AFPA). They are recognized by the NBFE and eight other agencies. It is their responsibility to make sure Karen has the training she needs to help you.

Ongoing continuing education as well as CPR/AED Red Cross training and First Aid augments the expertise of a good trainer.

Make an Appointment

It doesn't matter if you are training with someone or alone. You still need to write your workouts in an appointment book. Schedule fitness training before your week begins. Most importantly, do your best to keep to the schedule and try your best not to cancel. Setting the time aside will do two things. It keeps you from getting caught up in the schedule of work or school and slipping something else into your calendar. It is a huge reminder of your commitment to your continued health and wholeness.

Whether you workout for the joy of sweat or the looser waistband, social support is key to flourishing. People are programmed to bond with other people; their brains need social connections to keep everything firing. We have an innate propensity to exercise our capacities and explore our limitations. This healthy, playful sense of being is optimized when shared with others. Whether you chose to book time with a personal trainer, gym partner, or friend, understand that by being there for yourself and others—everything is not only changed for the better, it's changed for good.

28

Affirmations and Reminders

The refrigerator is a message center in many homes. Make a habit of leaving affirmations to support your powerful positive mindset. Set the motivational phrase "Be Fit!" as your screen saver or post a note that says, "Eat to Live!" Put sticky notes on your dashboard, your bathroom mirror, etc. Remind yourself that living your dreams means waking up to the new you.

Build Your Dreams

Field of Dreams is one of our favorite movies. The mysterious voice tells actor, Kevin Costner, "If you build it, they will come." Making changes within yourself is very much like this. You create your own world. Psychological researchers and theologians believe that your life and health are affected by your mindset. Your mind builds your reality. The physical world is the reflection of how and what you think. Your program will excel with a belief in the existence of God or a higher power.

People with a strong faith are better able to grapple with daily problems. Faith plays a compelling role in discouraging destructive behaviors by promoting self-worth and confidence. Believing that a higher power is aware of you and cares for you eliminates deep loneliness. Prayer and meditation help us to cope with stressful events and situations. Religious beliefs don't rely on facts in order to be accepted as truth. Faith can positively shape our mental wellbeing, bolster our immune system, and support other physiological aspects that influence our health.

Science has proven the importance of thoughts in healing and perception. People taking a placebo can get well if they believe they have the most powerful drug on the market today. Even when you think you have it all together there will be times you find yourself covered with a rash of old bad habits. After a stressful meeting you might be tempted to appease the grumbling gut with an order of onion rings, a chili dog and a root beer float. You rationalize that if you gobble big mouthfuls really quick it'll run right through your gut before your hips get wind of the extra calories. Nobody will be the wiser.

Except you know. When running up a hill, it's okay to stop and catch your breath. The hill isn't going any place—you are. Stopping is not falling behind. Picking back up the pace and climbing forward is an act of will. Keep moving and you'll reach the top. When you view a valley from the peak the extent of your trek is evident. There is no straight line connecting the two—the path is winding and sometimes appears to turn back on itself in order to bypass barriers. What matters most is that you and the peak are together.

A Different Kind of Scale

This is the only scale you need to consider. When earlier you chose a fitness level, we asked you to decide how you want to live your life.

What do you want your fitness level to be?

- A sleek, slim body with no wrinkles, dimples or bulges
- A concaved abdomen with a "six pack"
- Comments from people, such as, "Oh, you're so thin…" (and you *know* they are really jealous)
- Men (or women) stop on the street to watch you walk by

However, the trade-offs are:

- Having to work out for at least an hour 5-6 days a week.
- Always eating a restricted diet.
- energy levels varying from low to hyper.
- Joints hurting more and more as you age.

Or can you come to grips with a body that is part of a healthy and enjoyable lifestyle. You:

- Might have a little bulge under your bra on your back.
- Might have a little curve to your tummy.
- Won't draw attention from everyone on the streets.
- Won't look like you did when you were 25.

In exchange for these flaws you have a good time with friends and eat carefully and in moderation. You get to the gym three times a week and incorporate thoughtful life choices. You have high energy and your body doesn't ache as you age.

Now, if you don't care about the consequences of a long life after the battle has been waged on your body to keep very thin, then that is your choice. The alternative is to have to reconcile within your heart what you can live with now. The choices may lead to other issues in your body due to strict dieting and abuse of the skeletal structure.

Karen's body does not move as it should. One look at her spine and hips told the chiropractor she had been a power lifter before she ever opened her mouth to recite a case history. He knew it and she is reminded of it daily. Be smart and remember that people live a lot longer these days. You don't want to have more issues because of a strict discipline you incorporated in your life once upon a time.

29

Come Together

"A foolish man never asks directions."

~ *Author Unknown*

A positive self-concept and healthy environment ground wellness programs. Physical strength and a reasonable quotient of emotional intelligence are assets that support mindfulness and a healthy approach to weight loss.

Feel the Burn

Eating by rote is how many people buffer their feelings. Obviously what feels good to the taste buds doesn't cure mental anguish. Working out is often connected with looking inward. As you burn off excess fat, and sweat out the toxins, it's possible to release negative energy associated with bad thoughts and hurt feelings. Deal with them head on through your journal. If you are not able to handle depressing thoughts or anxiety consider seeking the help of a professional listener. That will boost your emotional IQ in a snap.

There is value in seeking help from a counselor or psychologist. Please consider doing this for yourself at some stage of your quest for fitness. As people, we are intricately connected to our bodies through our thoughts and feelings. A psychologist or licensed therapist can help you weed through your thoughts and questions.

If you are overwhelmed and under-esteemed or depressed and downhearted you are well advised to contact your family physician and ask for a counseling referral. Make the appointment and get yourself some professional help. You will be glad you did.

Positive reinforcement is the best way to guarantee success. Everybody wants to hear the roar of a crowd cheering, but you can never be sure all your feedback will be helpful. It's impossible to explain in words the true feelings you have about the journey you are undertaking. Don't even try. It will come out sounding canned, like something from a movie script.

Even telling someone how you got from point A to point B in your thoughts can be difficult. How do you expect to explain a lifetime of feelings about yourself and your desire to change that image? I advise you to hold your cards very close to your chest. Even telling your spouse at first can be frustrating because they have probably heard you promise to lose weight before.

Avoid always relying on your family, spouse, or closest friend for ZWL support. They will have all the best intentions in the world, but they are not equipped to handle your needs. They have needs and demons of their own. Choose a professional or steep yourself deeply in a prayer life for support.

Supreme Beings

Like so many successful programs that change peoples lives, there is the absolute need to rely on a higher power. Whatever your belief and practice you will need to rely on that for support with The ZWL.

Refrain from telling everyone about your plan to get fit and trim. You might think you will do better if lots of people know you are trying. Then you won't cheat on your diet. It doesn't work that way. Say nothing, even after they notice, and they will.

As your fitness level improves, your brain and the world will notice. At about the same time, if you have been meditating and practicing mindfulness, you will be increasingly aware of the world. Your senses will be enhanced and your awareness will be bountiful. Not everyone will be excited; some will say nothing out of jealousy. Others will ask for your secret.

Trying to explain your routine to people may introduce you to the fitness controversy and make you question the path you are on. Your friends and family will tell you what they read, what they heard on television, and that may build doubt and confusion in your life.

This is far too personal a quest for you to share every aspect of your fitness program with anyone willing to listen. This book is designed to help you formulate your own fitness program. Your story will not apply to someone else. In the meantime, keep it to yourself and accept the compliments with the knowledge that you earned it. Be gracious and say, "Thank you."

Positive personal relationships are part of a healthy psyche. Brains are deeply social. Brain scans have shown that social pain is as real as physical pain. The Beatle's wisdom holds true in the fitness world too. "We get by with a little help from our friends."

Invite a close friend to share the quest for fitness. Discuss the benefits and options of working out together. Review and arrange your schedules to find openings to meet at a gym or to go for walks. Even if you are at different fitness levels, a training partner is an invaluable support. Friends can help us to avoid negative situations ("let's meet for wings and beers after work") and approach positive situations ("let's do the gym during lunch"). However, positive personal relationships are essential for good physical and mental health.

Benefits of Sweat

If your friends decline the invitation, make a new friend at the gym. You don't have to spend time with this person outside the gym—think of it as a "friend with bene-sweats" relationship. Take your time, ramp up your social awareness of the body language expressed by other people at the gym when you are there. There's a certain unspoken etiquette in fitness centers. A woman jogging on the treadmill wearing iPod earphones or reading a magazine on the stationary bike isn't looking for casual conversation. A guy with a hundred pounds of metal poised above his head doesn't want to talk baseball. When some people are in the zone of a grueling workout they avoid all social contact—even eye contact. Be sensitive to their space.

Then again, there are women who bound into the gym with shrieks of delight that it's *finally* time for the group Pilates session. Surely there is at least one among them who would enjoy working out with a buddy on the classes off days. The need to be social is a powerful motivation. It's surprising how many times you'll show up at the gym because you know someone's waiting for you.

Tom, a healthy guy in his mid-20s, describes his connection to the gym as the social center in his world. Besides working out at least three times per week he has networked business-marketing connections. He's made new friends and dated other clients. He is considering moving closer to the gym when his apartment lease expires because it will be easier to pop in for a quick "kick out the jams" and, he grinned, "you never know what social opportunities will appear."

Start with your regular routine. You'll notice certain people are there every time you are. You ask to "work in" with them and when they are resting between sets, you do a set, chat a little, and say goodbye. The more often you do this the more fun a workout can be.

One day the timing will be right and you can ask the person if they would like to work out together. "Have you ever been interested in a training partner?" You could also say, "It sure is easier to drag myself in here when I know I have someone to work out with." Try this one on them, "That was a great workout! Let's do it again sometime." When the next time becomes the next time you'll both be into a routine that helps maintain each other's focus.

A training partnership is a mutually beneficial situation. You feed off each other's energy, offer mutual encouragement, and positive reinforcement. You motivate each other. You develop a sharp eye that picks up signs of improvement in endurance and appearance. Long-term training partners have a special relationship. Generally the conversation is upbeat and interesting which makes time appear to move quickly, before you know it, the session is over.

We're wired to respond to others in ways that are automatic and involuntary. That's why group workouts and classes are so effective. When you see other people's movement, sense their inner energy, and feel the power of bodies growing stronger—you'll do the same. We are mirrors reflecting each other's pain, pleasure, passion, and progress. The pleasure achieved by a good workout transforms social pain to happiness.

30

This Moment Now

Set to Succeed

What do we do about our failures to achieve? We might deceive ourselves. Perhaps we follow the healthy routine and then suddenly succumb to that horrible craving for something that isn't a good choice—and we become the Bernie Madoff of our own demise—swindling our personal health. We break our own rules and allow food to gain advantage. We escape wellness and defraud our own fitness.

Weakness is as much a part of human psychology as is strength. Without weakness we have no sense of strength. They are flip sides of the same nickel. One of the greatest things about success is that we often work hard to achieve because we are afraid to fail. ZWL is learning to achieve and maintain balance. We all want to win because we are afraid to lose. In order to understand success we study failure. By understanding loss we prize what we have. And so, if to be human is to err, and to play fair is to know cheating, let's accept that every now and then you're going to bamboozle your fitness plan. Here are a few recommendations on how to have a successful, life altering cheat session.

The minute you find yourself thinking about eating something that is not a good choice—pause for a mini-second. Breathe slowly and become conscious of that very movement. Visualize the source of your longing. Blow out the desire. Breathe in gratitude for inner strength and self-discipline.

Notice your environment. Are the people you are with the ones you usually see day to day? Is this a special event of some kind? Did you eat today or are you hungry? Why now? If you are able, write down your feelings and decide if you want to eat this unfriendly food.

If you were walking forward when the thought arose—take a step to the right or left and visualize stepping away from your craving. If you're sitting in traffic—change the radio channel and sing about the craving to the tune of whatever is playing. Sounds ridiculous? So is your craving.

If at all possible wait a day before you break down and eat this "food verboten". Often the desire comes because you are in an environment where you used to eat that food. Let's say you have been invited to a birthday party for an old friend. For many of us who never met a dessert we didn't love, the southern belle approach is always best; eat *before* you go to the party. You will have more control! If you haven't seen these friends recently, you might show up, order a glass of water or tea and prepare to "be good".

Moderation

Don't make a public party proclamation that you are dieting. They don't care and frankly, it's a bit of rain on their parade. Thank anyone who notices changes in your body but don't expand on all the hard mental, physical and emotional investments you've made in your fitness program. Ask about them! Get them to talk and you listen, really pay attention. The focus on another may be all that needed to quell your appetite. When you eat just keep a simple mantra, "Moderation."

If the table wins, and just like in Vegas the odds are it will, don't condemn yourself. Make your next meal a healthy one. Write about it in your food journal. If you get stuck on visions of pasta alfredo or ice cream try to analyze your thinking and cravings. Thinking is rational—cravings are impulsive. Thinking takes time and that often short circuits the percussive burst of a madcap impulse.

Understand that dependency and addiction are talking. Your physical body may have eaten the unfriendly food for so long that it's built up a tolerance. It craves greater portions to get the same pleasure that a little nibble stimulated before. The power of understanding empowers you to deny the beast what it wants. Keep it under control. Even if it means pacing the room, eating 1000 calories of vegetables and fruit, and drinking enough water to keep you up all night in the bathroom. Be strong.

Although you are healing and becoming a new person, realize that the little fat girl or boy is still inside you. That isn't all bad! Having that person within makes you who you are today. Make peace with painful aspects of your past. You have experiences other people can never realize, and because of them you have so much more to offer. Live and be the example of fitness renewed!

You have grown as your body has shrunk. Nobody is as good as you being you. Nobody needs to acknowledge what you have been through. Nobody will be as strong of a you as you have become. Please attend to this new and improved You with great kindness and compassion. Be good to yourself. Rather than let old, outdated opinions of yourself get in the way of being You, accept the gift of not knowing what the future holds. Celebrate being "You" and knowing there is no other place or time that is better than now.

Another sure way to fail is to tell yourself you are never going to eat ice cream, or never going to have pasta. The only thing you'll be able to think about is what you can't have. It fills your mind and you won't be happy until you eat it, and often a ton of it. We are creatures of habits and desire neither restraint nor denial. We crave what we are denied—that leaves us with the power to choose among an abundance of healthy options. Choose moderation and reason—choose to be fit.

You can, however, decide to serve a moderate or small plate of pasta with a large platter of vegetables. An Italian friend always serves a green vegetable such as simmered peas and baby onions as a side to her marinara sauce and spaghetti. Your food prep can also include a moderate work out. Go to the gym and walk the treadmill for 20 minutes followed by 10 minutes on the elliptical. Don't worry about creating too big of an appetite—the physical workout will balance your hunger. Consider short and concise workouts as part of your meal preparation and you'll reap a series of successes. Everybody can live with one success after another, especially if they come a minute at a time.

Now is the Moment

ZWL is not a program built on promises. It is centered within the mind and body with a keen appreciation for what is now. Humans are gifted with the ability to perceive the abstract concepts concerning the future. Belief in a better tomorrow is harnessed through ZWL as a stimulus to making our brains and bodies change is ways that are for better and for good.

We can take back a pair of slacks that don't fit. We only have one opportunity to return our bodies from where they came. All returns are final. In the meantime, we have the motive, opportunity, and power to become swifter. Stronger legs can take us further along the path. We can soar higher towards the sun. Our workouts will strengthen our spines and support us with less pain on the long walk towards tomorrow.

Swifter, higher, stronger are ample descriptions of people who see themselves clearly and calmly as fit, healthy, and just about right size to make it though this life.

> *"The time will come when with elation you'll greet yourself arriving at your own door, in your own mirror, and each will smile at the other's welcome and say, Sit here. Eat. You will love again the stranger who was yourself."*
>
> ~ *Derek Wolcott*

> *"I'd rather pick daisies than push them up any day."*
>
> ~ *JAL*

Appendix

Start Worksheet

This exercise will help you prepare for an appointment with your family doctor. When you make your appointment ask to have blood work done in advance of your appointment so you can discuss the results with your doctor. Ask for COMPLETE blood work: thyroid, cholesterol, triglycerides, etc. Request as much as your doctor thinks is necessary and the insurance company will cover.

Think of every question you can, write them within this worksheet, and be sure to take this page with you. Do not skimp on this. Tell him everything about yourself and your plans too!

Physician: _____

Date of Appointment: _____

Physicians Phone: _____

Date for Lab Work: _____

Questions for your physician:

_____

_____

_____

_____

_____

_____

Regular physical activity is fun and healthy, and increasingly more people are starting to become more active every day. Being more active is very safe for most people. However, some people should check with their physician before they start becoming more physically active. **Please complete this form as accurately and completely as possible.**

PAR-Q Form

Please circle YES or No to the following.

Has your doctor ever said that you have a heart condition and recommended only medically supervised physical activity? YES NO

Do you frequently have pains in your chest when you perform physical activity? YES NO

Have you had chest pain when you were not doing physical activity? YES NO

Have you had a stroke? YES NO

Do you lose your balance due to dizziness or do you ever lose consciousness? YES NO

Do you have a bone, joint or any other health problem that causes you pain or limitations that must be addressed when developing an exercise program (i.e. diabetes, osteoporosis, high blood pressure, high cholesterol, arthritis, anorexia, bulimia, anemia, epilepsy, respiratory ailments, back problems, etc.)? YES NO

Are you pregnant now or have given birth within the last 6 months? YES NO

Do you have asthma or exercise induced asthma? YES NO

Do you have low blood sugar levels (hypoglycemia)? YES NO

Do you have diabetes? YES NO

Have you had a recent surgery? YES NO

If you have marked YES to any of the previous questions, please elaborate below:

_____

_____

_____

PAR-Q Form (cont.)

Do you take any medications, either prescription or non-prescription,   YES   NO
on a regular basis?

What are the medications for? _____

_____

How does this medication affect your ability to exercise or achieve
your fitness goals?

_____

_____

Please note: If your health changes such that you could then answer YES to any of the
above questions, tell your trainer/coach. Ask whether you should change your physical
activity plan.

☐ I have read, understood, and completed the questionnaire. Any questions I had were
answered to my full satisfaction.

Physical Activity Readiness Questionnaire (PAR Q)

The PAR-Q was created by the British Columbia Ministry of Health
and the Multidisciplinary Board on Exercise. This form was adopted
directly from the ACSM Standards and Guidelines for Health and
Fitness Facilities.

Starting Measurements

Some of the measurements below you will have to do on your own or at your gym. The blood pressure and heart rate you can get from the nurse in your doctor's office. Get your spouse or a friend to do the others. Notice we are not using a scale to measure. That's because you will be building muscle, which weighs more than fat. Trust me, you can find the scale staying in the same place while you drop in clothing size! If you prefer to weigh on a scale, always use the same one and do it no more than once every two weeks.

Today's Date: _____

RESTING MEASURES

Blood Pressure _____

Heart Rate _____

Target heart rate 55%_____ to 85% _____

BODY COMPOSITION
(This can be done at your gym. It's not a necessary measurement)

Skin fold measurements _____

Weight: _____ (if you must)

Triceps _____

Bicep _____

Back _____

Waist _____

Total % body fat _____

Bioelectrical impedance _____

Starting Measurements (cont.)

GIRTH MEASUREMENTS

This is best when done by another person.

_____ Chest

_____ Abdomen
(Measure around your middle meeting at your
belly button)

_____ Hips
(Be sure to move lower and encompass your buttocks)

_____ Right Thigh
(Measure a palm's width above the kneecap—a full
width of the hand with fingers extended. Be sure to
the tape measure is above the little finger. OR measure
6" up from your kneecap and then measure around
your thigh.)

MUSCULAR ENDURANCE

Do as many as you can of each of these exercises. Push-ups can be
done against the wall if you are not strong enough to do any on the
floor. If you can do none of them, be sure to write "0". Now, look
at how much you will be able to improve!

Push Ups _____

Pull Ups _____

Crunches _____

Food Journal

Our recommendation is to get a small notebook so you can write things down for a minimum of two weeks. This journal page will help you understand how to journal. After you have listed foods you need to be aware of how the food makes you feel.

Watch for gas, indigestion, rash, mood swings, pain, other digestive issues

Write down how you felt when you woke and how the food affected you throughout the day.

Below is an example of a journal page:

Thursday, May 05, 2011
4:00 a.m. woke and had oatmeal for breakfast. Coffee.
    Water, vitamins
Stretched, tight with back ache early. Body very stiff and sore.
    Almost can't walk. High carbohydrate dinner. Spaghetti
    and meatballs. Can't handle pasta?????
6:00 left for work. Energy level about an 8/10 clear head
9:00 snack. Handful of peanuts (aprox 2 tbsp).
    Felt clear-headed still
11:00 ready for lunch but have to work. Had apple
    to hold over. Tense.
1:00 p.m. late lunch. Salad lettuce, spinach, peppers, grape
    tomatoes, other veggies. Sunflower seeds. chicken (4oz). feta
    cheese (2 tbsp). 2 tbsp raisins. Dressing sesame ginger
    (2g fat/serving)
4:00 cheese and crackers...soft lite cheese with gluten free
    crackers (6)
    Restless for dinner. Should have had more protein at lunch?
    Waited too long to have lunch.
7:00 Shrimp stir fry. Veggies (broccoli, spinach peppers onions,
    green beans). Sauted in some olive oil

As you begin this process you will discover the foods that help your body work to its optimum performance!

Taking a Closer Look

Today's Date: _____

Look at yourself in the mirror. Make no judgments, but answer the following questions.

- Is this the body you remembered from years ago?

- Does this body look like it's around for the long haul?

- Are you ready to do the work to make it better?

Journal in the spaced provided below. This is your private reflection on the situation you find yourself in right now. Be candid and honest but don't beat yourself up!

Setting Your Goals

This Step Really Counts

Think about your deepest desires. Often the stories, movies or books we read will give us ideas which lead us toward discovering our own purpose in life. What is it you want to do when you grow up? We won't be happy until we're doing that "thing" which makes our soul soar. How do you want to help the world? I don't mean helping on an international or national level. I mean helping your own little community, block, or school. How do you want to be remembered?

Start making notes in the space provided below. Continue your thoughts in your journal and focus on the words that make you feel excited. I call this a top-secret section because this is the kind of thing you share with no one really. It is between you and God and it is sacred. Build your dream and others will see it soon enough. You may choose to put goals for your body and workouts in this segment.

Physical	Mental	Spiritual
_____	_____	_____
_____	_____	_____
_____	_____	_____
_____	_____	_____
_____	_____	_____
_____	_____	_____
_____	_____	_____
_____	_____	_____

About the Authors

Karen Fili Sullivan is an AFPA (American Fitness Professionals and Associates) Certified Personal Trainer and Rehabilitation Expert near St. Louis, Missouri. An expert at riding the diet roller coaster, she broke that cycle with the ZWL Method. In her home gym and through Cyber Space coaching she mediates a path to a better body and healthier life. Her balance comes from reading, writing, walking the beach and enjoying time with her husband David, sons Brenden and Jared and her yellow lab, Hank.

Follow her at
http://karenfilisullivan.com
Twitter @kfilisullivan
karenfilisullivan@gmail.com

Jeri Levesque has been training with Karen and following ZWL for three years. She is an avid sailor, reader, gourmet cook, writer, and lover of all things to do with boats and the sea. As the mother of three, grandmother of four, and wife of George for 41 years, she needs to stay fit and centered in order to keep her promise to dance at all of her grandkids' weddings.

Follow her at http://Jalsails.wordpress.com/

Made in the USA
Columbia, SC
08 March 2018